THE CERTIFIED INTERNAL AUDITOR®

MODEL EXAM QUESTIONS 2004

Published By
The Institute of Internal Auditors
Research Foundation

Disclosure

Copyright © 2004 by The Institute of Internal Auditors Research Foundation, 247 Maitland Avenue, Altamonte Springs, Florida 32701-4201. All rights reserved. Printed in the United States of America. No part of this publication may be reproduced, stored in a retrieval system, or transmitted in any form by any means — electronic, mechanical, photocopying, recording, or otherwise — without prior written permission of the publisher.

The IIA publishes this document for informational and educational purposes. This document is intended to provide information, but is not a substitute for legal or accounting advice. The IIA does not provide such advice and makes no warranty as to any legal or accounting results through its publication of this document. When legal or accounting issues arise, professional assistance should be sought and retained.

The Professional Practices Framework for Internal Auditing (PPF) was designed by The IIA Board of Directors' Guidance Task Force to appropriately organize the full range of existing and developing practice guidance for the profession. Based on the definition of internal auditing, the PPF comprises *Ethics* and *Standards, Practice Advisories,* and *Development and Practice Aids,* and paves the way to world-class internal auditing.

This guidance fits into the Framework under the heading *Development and Practice Aids*.

ISBN 0-89413-530-9
05619 October 2005
Second Printing

Foreword

Since the Board of Regents of The Institute of Internal Auditors (IIA) initiated the Certified Internal Auditor® (CIA®) program in December 1972, the CIA examination has occasionally been revised to reflect changes in the profession and changes in testing methodology.

Model Exam Questions 2004 reflects content changes due to the modifications to the CIA syllabus effective with the May 2004 testing cycle. **Model Exam Questions 2004 includes only 100 questions per part, while beginning in May 2004, the CIA exam will contain 125 questions per part.** The 125 questions on the actual exam parts will include up to 25 unscored questions, which will be used for research purposes. These unscored questions will be interspersed with the scored questions and will not be identified as unscored questions. Candidates should therefore answer all 125 questions to the best of their ability.

Model Exam Questions 2004 is intended as a means of familiarizing interested parties with the content and format of the CIA exam. It is not meant to replace the material supplied by any of the third-party providers of CIA exam review materials. The questions in this publication, whether new or adapted from earlier CIA exams, are simply representative of the format, length, and content of questions that a CIA candidate can expect to see on future exams. A current or future CIA exam candidate's success or failure in answering these questions should not be taken as any form of guarantee of that candidate's results on an actual CIA exam.

If there are any significant changes in the format or content of the CIA exam in the future, the Certification Department will make those changes known through our Web site (**www.theiia.org**) and/or through mailings to current CIA candidates.

For further information on the CIA program, please visit the "Certification" heading on the Web site listed above, or contact The IIA's Customer Service Center for a brochure:

The Institute of Internal Auditors
Customer Service Center
247 Maitland Avenue
Altamonte Springs, Florida 32701-4201, USA
Phone: +1-407-937-1111
Fax: +1-407-937-1101
E-mail: custserv@theiia.org

Contents

Foreword iii

Topics Tested vii

Part I: The Internal Audit Activity's Role in Governance, Risk, and Control
Model Exam Questions .... I - 1
Solutions (with cross-reference to topics tested) .... I - 17

Part II: Conducting the Internal Audit Engagement
Model Exam Questions .... II - 1
Solutions (with cross-reference to topics tested) .... II - 17

Part III: Business Analysis and Information Technology
Model Exam Questions .... III - 1
Solutions (with cross-reference to topics tested) .... III - 13

Part IV: Business Management Skills
Model Exam Questions .... IV - 1
Solutions (with cross-reference to topics tested) .... IV - 13

v

Topics Tested on the Certified Internal Auditor (CIA) Examination

The following pages provide detailed topic outlines for each part of the Certified Internal Auditor (CIA) examination. Candidates are advised to plan their study based on the detailed topic outlines, rather than limiting their study to those topics that appear on the enclosed *Model Exam Questions*.

The CIA examination tests knowledge of the specified topics at two levels of competency, as defined below:

Awareness – Candidate exhibits awareness of basic facts/terminology and an appreciation of the broad nature and fundamentals of the topic being tested. Candidates are not expected to have detailed knowledge of topics listed.

Proficiency – Candidate is able to exhibit the ability to apply specific knowlede to areas likely to be encountered and to deal with these areas without extensive recourse to technical research or assistance. Candidates are expected to demonstrate a thorough understanding of the principles, practices, and procedures of the topic being tested.

The detailed topic outlines which follow note the required level of competency for each topic area.

Please note that the CIA exam tests The IIA's *Professional Practices Framework* (PPF). The PPF consists of three categories of guidance. The first category (Mandatory Guidance) consists of core materials: the *IIA Code of Ethics* and the *International Standards for the Professional Practice of Internal Auditing* (with the Glossary). These will be tested as mandatory. (Example: Which of the following is required according to the *Standards*?) Guidance in the second category (*Practice Advisories*) is strongly recommended and endorsed by The IIA but is not mandatory. While the *Practice Advisories* are not mandatory, candidates are expected to know them at the proficiency level. In responding to exam questions, candidates should note that *Practice Advisories* will be treated as correct practices and will be accepted as the appropriate method of performance. The third category of guidance (Development & Practice Aids) will not be specifically tested as part of the PPF. However, some of these materials may be used as references for exam questions on the topic areas that they cover.

PART I: THE INTERNAL AUDIT ACTIVITY'S ROLE IN GOVERNANCE, RISK, AND CONTROL

A. **Comply with The IIA's Attribute Standards (15-25%) [Proficiency level]**
   1. Define purpose, authority, and responsibility of the internal audit activity
      a. Determine if the purpose, authority, and responsibility of the internal audit activity are clearly documented and approved.
      b. Determine if the purpose, authority, and responsibility of the internal audit activity are communicated to the engagement clients
      c. Demonstrate an understanding of the purpose, authority, and responsibility of the internal audit activity
   2. Maintain independence and objectivity
      a. Foster independence
         1) Understand organizational independence
         2) Recognize the importance of organizational independence
         3) Determine if the internal audit activity is properly aligned to achieve organizational independence
      b. Foster objectivity
         1) Establish policies to promote objectivity
         2) Assess individual objectivity
         3) Maintain individual objectivity
         4) Recognize and mitigate impairments to independence and objectivity
   3. Determine if the required knowledge, skills, and competencies are available
      a. Understand the knowledge, skills, and competencies that an internal auditor needs to possess
      b. Identify the knowledge, skills, and competencies required to fulfill the responsibilities of the internal audit activity
   4. Develop and/or procure the necessary knowledge, skills, and competencies collectively required by the internal audit activity
   5. Exercise due professional care
   6. Promote continuing professional development
      a. Develop and implement a plan for continuing professional development for internal audit staff
      b. Enhance individual competency through continuing professional development
   7. Promote quality assurance and improvement of the internal audit activity
      a. Establish and maintain a quality assurance and improvement program
      b. Monitor the effectiveness of the quality assurance and improvement program
      c. Report the results of the quality assurance and improvement program to the board or other governing body
      d. Conduct quality assurance procedures and recommend improvements to the performance of the internal audit activity
   8. Abide by and promote compliance with The IIA Code of Ethics.

B. **Establish a Risk-based Plan to Determine the Priorities of the Internal Audit Activity (15-25%) [Proficiency level]**
   1. Establish a framework for assessing risk
   2. Use the framework to:
      a. Identify sources of potential engagements (e.g., audit universe, management request, regulatory mandate)
      b. Assess organization-wide risk
      c. Solicit potential engagement topics from various sources
      d. Collect and analyze data on proposed engagements
      e. Rank and validate risk priorities

(CONTINUED ON NEXT PAGE)

3. Identify internal audit resource requirements
4. Coordinate the internal audit activity's efforts with:
   a. External auditor
   b. Regulatory oversight bodies
   c. Other internal assurance functions (e.g., health and safety department)
5. Select engagements
   a. Participate in the engagement selection process
   b. Select engagements
   c. Communicate and obtain approval of the engagement plan from board

C. **Understand the Internal Audit Activity's Role in Organizational Governance (10-20%) [Proficiency level]**
   1. Obtain board's approval of audit charter
   2. Communicate plan of engagements
   3. Report significant audit issues
   4. Communicate key performance indicators to board on a regular basis
   5. Discuss areas of significant risk
   6. Support board in enterprise-wide risk assessment
   7. Review the positioning of the internal audit function within the risk management framework within the organization.
   8. Monitor compliance with the corporate code of conduct/business practices
   9. Report on the effectiveness of the control framework
   10. Assist board in assessing the independence of the external auditor
   11. Assess ethical climate of the board
   12. Assess ethical climate of the organization
   13. Assess compliance with policies in specific areas (e.g., derivatives)
   14. Assess organization's reporting mechanism to the board
   15. Conduct follow-up and report on management response to regulatory body reviews
   16. Conduct follow-up and report on management response to external audit
   17. Assess the adequacy of the performance measurement system, achievement of corporate objective
   18. Support a culture of fraud awareness and encourage the reporting of improprieties

D. **Perform Other Internal Audit Roles and Responsibilities (0-10%) [Proficiency level]**
   1. Ethics/Compliance
      a. Investigate and recommend resolution for ethics/compliance complaints
      b. Determine disposition of ethics violations
      c. Foster healthy ethical climate
      d. Maintain and administer business conduct policy (e.g., conflict of interest)
      e. Report on compliance
   2. Risk Management
      a. Develop and implement an organization-wide risk and control framework
      b. Coordinate enterprise-wide risk assessment
      c. Report corporate risk assessment to board
      d. Review business continuity planning process
   3. Privacy
      a. Determine privacy vulnerabilities
      b. Report on compliance
   4. Information or physical security
      a. Determine security vulnerabilities
      b. Determine disposition of security violations
      c. Report on compliance

(CONTINUED ON NEXT PAGE)

E. Governance, Risk, and Control Knowledge Elements (15-25%)
1. Corporate governance principles [Awareness level]
2. Alternative control frameworks [Awareness level]
3. Risk vocabulary and concepts [Proficiency level]
4. Risk management techniques [Proficiency level]
5. Risk/control implications of different organizational structures [Proficiency level]
6. Risk/control implications of different leadership styles [Awareness level]
7. Change management [Awareness level]
8. Conflict management [Awareness level]
9. Management control techniques [Proficiency level]
10. Types of control (e.g., preventive, detective, input, output) [Proficiency level]

F. Plan Engagements (15-25%) [Proficiency level]
1. Initiate preliminary communication with engagement client
2. Conduct a preliminary survey of the area of engagement
    a. Obtain input from engagement client
    b. Perform analytical reviews
    c. Perform benchmarking
    d. Conduct interviews
    e. Review prior audit reports and other relevant documentation
    f. Map processes
    g. Develop checklists
3. Complete a detailed risk assessment of area (prioritize or evaluate risk/control factors)
4. Coordinate audit engagement efforts with
    a. External auditor
    b. Regulatory oversight bodies
5. Establish/refine engagement objectives and identify/finalize the scope of engagement
6. Identify or develop criteria for assurance engagements (criteria against which to audit)
7. Consider the potential for fraud when planning an engagement
    a. Be knowledgeable of the risk factors and red flags of fraud
    b. Identify common types of fraud associated with the engagement area.
    c. Determine if risk of fraud requires special consideration when conducting an engagement
8. Determine engagement procedures
9. Determine the level of staff and resources needed for the engagement.
10. Establish adequate planning and supervision of the engagement.
11. Prepare engagement work program

Format: 125 multiple-choice questions

PART II: CONDUCTING THE INTERNAL AUDIT ENGAGEMENT

A. **Conduct Engagements (25-35%) [Proficiency level]**
   1. Research and apply appropriate standards:
      a. IIA Professional Practices Framework (Code of Ethics, Standards, Practice Advisories)
      b. Other professional, legal, and regulatory standards
   2. Maintain an awareness of the potential for fraud when conducting an engagement
      a. Notice indicators or symptoms of fraud
      b. Design appropriate engagement steps to address significant risk of fraud
      c. Employ audit tests to detect fraud
      d. Determine if any suspected fraud merits investigation
   3. Collect data
   4. Evaluate the relevance, sufficiency and competence of evidence
   5. Analyze and interpret data
   6. Develop workpapers
   7. Review workpapers
   8. Communicate interim progress
   9. Draw conclusions
   10. Develop recommendations when appropriate
   11. Report engagement results
      a. Conduct exit conference
      b. Prepare report or other communication
      c. Approve engagement report
      d. Determine distribution of report
      e. Obtain management response to report
   12. Conduct client satisfaction survey
   13. Complete performance appraisals of engagement staff

B. **Conduct Specific Engagements (25-35%) [Proficiency level]**
   1. Conduct assurance engagements
      a. Fraud investigation
         1) Determine appropriate parties to be involved with investigation
         2) Establish facts and extent of fraud (e.g., interviews, interrogations, and data analysis)
         3) Report outcomes to appropriate parties
         4) Complete a process review to improve controls to prevent fraud and recommend changes
      b. Risk and control self-assessment
         1) Facilitated approach
            a) Client-facilitated
            b) Audit-facilitated
         2) Questionnaire approach
         3) Self-certification approach
      c. Audits of third parties and contract auditing
      d. Quality audit engagements
      e. Due diligence audit engagements
      f. Security audit engagements
      g. Privacy audit engagements
      h. Performance (key performance indicators) audit engagements
      i. Operational (efficiency and effectiveness) audit engagements
      j. Financial audit engagements

(CONTINUED ON NEXT PAGE)

        k.   Information technology (IT) audit engagements
            1)   Operating systems
                a)   Mainframe
                b)   Workstations
                c)   Server
            2)   Application development
                a)   Application authentication
                b)   Systems development methodology
                c)   Change control
                d)   End user computing
            3)   Data and network communications/connections (e.g., LAN, VAN, and WAN)
            4)   Voice communications
            5)   System security (e.g., firewalls, access control)
            6)   Contingency planning
            7)   Databases
            8)   Functional areas of IT operations (e.g., data center operations)
            9)   Web infrastructure
            10) Software licensing
            11) Electronic funds transfer (EFT)/Electronic data interchange (EDI)
            12) e-Commerce
            13) Information protection/viruses
            14) Encryption
            15) Enterprise-wide resource planning (ERP) software (e.g., SAP R/3)
        l.   Compliance audit engagements
    2.   Conduct consulting engagements
        a.   Internal control training
        b.   Business process review
        c.   Benchmarking
        d.   Information technology (IT) and systems development.
        e.   Design of performance measurement systems

C.   Monitor Engagement Outcomes (5-15%) [Proficiency level]
    1.   Determine appropriate follow-up activity by the internal audit activity
    2.   Identify appropriate method to monitor engagement outcomes
    3.   Conduct follow-up activity
    4.   Communicate monitoring plan and results

D.   Fraud Knowledge Elements (5-15%)
    1.   Discovery sampling [Awareness level]
    2.   Interrogation techniques [Awareness level]
    3.   Forensic auditing [Awareness level]
    4.   Use of computers in analyzing data [Proficiency level]
    5.   Red flags [Proficiency level]
    6.   Types of fraud [Proficiency level]

E.   Engagement Tools (15-25%)
    1.   Sampling [Awareness level]
        a.   Nonstatistical (judgmental)
        b.   Statistical
    2.   Statistical analyses (process control techniques) [Awareness level]
    3.   Data gathering tools [Proficiency level]
        a.   Interviewing
        b.   Questionnaires
        c.   Checklists

(CONTINUED ON NEXT PAGE)

4. Analytical review techniques [Proficiency level]
   a. Ratio estimation
   b. Variance analysis (e.g., budget vs. actual)
   c. Other reasonableness tests
5. Observation [Proficiency level]
6. Problem solving [Proficiency level]
7. Risk and control self-assessment (CSA) [Awareness level]
8. Computerized audit tools and techniques [Proficiency level]
   a. Embedded audit modules
   b. Data extraction techniques
   c. Generalized audit software (e.g., ACL, IDEA)
   d. Spreadsheet analysis
   e. Automated workpapers (e.g., Lotus Notes, Auditor Assistant)
9. Process mapping including flowcharting [Proficiency level]

Format: 125 multiple-choice questions

PART III: BUSINESS ANALYSIS AND INFORMATION TECHNOLOGY

A. **Business Processes (15-25%)**
   1. Quality management (e.g., TQM) [Awareness level]
   2. The International Organization for Standardization (ISO) framework [Awareness level]
   3. Forecasting [Awareness level]
   4. Project management techniques [Proficiency level]
   5. Business process analysis (e.g., workflow analysis and bottleneck management, theory of constraints) [Proficiency level]
   6. Inventory management techniques and concepts [Proficiency level]
   7. Marketing- pricing objectives and policies [Awareness level]
   8. Marketing- supply chain management [Awareness level]
   9. Human Resources (Individual performance management and measurement; supervision; environmental factors that affect performance; facilitation techniques; personnel sourcing/staffing; training and development; safety) [Proficiency level]
   10. Balanced scorecard [Awareness level]

B. **Financial Accounting and Finance (15-25%)**
   1. Basic concepts and underlying principles of financial accounting (e.g., statements, terminology, relationships) [Proficiency level]
   2. Intermediate concepts of financial accounting (e.g., bonds, leases, pensions, intangible assets, R&D) [Awareness level]
   3. Advanced concepts of financial accounting (e.g., consolidation, partnerships, foreign currency transactions) [Awareness level]
   4. Financial statement analysis [Proficiency level]
   5. Cost of capital evaluation [Awareness level]
   6. Types of debt and equity [Awareness level]
   7. Financial instruments (e.g., derivatives) [Awareness level]
   8. Cash management (treasury functions) [Awareness level]
   9. Valuation models [Awareness level]
      a. Inventory valuation
      b. Business valuation
   10. Business development life cycles [Awareness level]

C. **Managerial Accounting (10-20%)**
   1. Cost concepts (e.g., absorption, variable, fixed) [Proficiency level]
   2. Capital budgeting [Awareness level]
   3. Operating budget [Proficiency level]
   4. Transfer pricing [Awareness level]
   5. Cost-volume-profit analysis [Awareness level]
   6. Relevant cost [Awareness level]
   7. Costing systems (e.g., activity-based, standard) [Awareness level]
   8. Responsibility accounting [Awareness level]

D. **Regulatory, Legal, and Economics (5-15%) [Awareness level]**
   1. Impact of government legislation and regulation on business
   2. Trade legislation and regulations
   3. Taxation schemes
   4. Contracts
   5. Nature and rules of legal evidence
   6. Key economic indicators

(CONTINUED ON NEXT PAGE)

E. Information Technology (IT) (30-40%) [Awareness level]
1. Control frameworks (e.g., SAC, COBIT)
2. Data and network communications/connections (e.g., LAN, VAN, and WAN)
3. Electronic funds transfer (EFT)
4. e-Commerce
5. Electronic data interchange (EDI)
6. Functional areas of IT operations (e.g., data center operations)
7. Encryption
8. Information protection (e.g., viruses, privacy)
9. Evaluate investment in IT (cost of ownership)
10. Enterprise-wide resource planning (ERP) software (e.g., SAP R/3)
11. Operating systems
12. Application development
13. Voice communications
14. Contingency planning
15. Systems security (e.g., firewalls, access control)
16. Databases
17. Software licensing
18. Web infrastructure

Format: 125 multiple-choice questions

PART IV: BUSINESS MANAGEMENT SKILLS

A. **Strategic Management (20-30%) [Awareness level]**
   1. Global analytical techniques
      a. Structural analysis of industries
      b. Competitive strategies (e.g., Porter's model)
      c. Competitive analysis
      d. Market signals
      e. Industry evolution
   2. Industry environments
      a. Competitive strategies related to:
         1) Fragmented industries
         2) Emerging industries
         3) Declining industries
      b. Competition in global industries
         1) Sources/impediments
         2) Evolution of global markets
         3) Strategic alternatives
         4) Trends affecting competition
   3. Strategic decisions
      a. Analysis of integration strategies
      b. Capacity expansion
      c. Entry into new businesses
   4. Portfolio techniques of competitive analysis
   5. Product life cycles

B. **Global Business Environments (15-25%) [Awareness level]**
   1. Cultural/legal/political environments
      a. Balancing global requirements and local imperatives
      b. Global mindsets (personal characteristics/competencies)
      c. Sources and methods for managing complexities and contradictions
      d. Managing multicultural teams
   2. Economic/financial environments
      a. Global, multinational, international, and multilocal compared and contrasted
      b. Requirements for entering the global market place
      c. Creating organizational adaptability
      d. Managing training and development.

C. **Organizational Behavior (15-25%) [Awareness level]**
   1. Motivation
      a. Relevance and implication of various theories
      b. Impact of job design, rewards, work schedules, etc.
   2. Communication
      a. The process
      b. Organizational dynamics
      c. Impact of computerization
   3. Performance
      a. Productivity
      b. Effectiveness
   4. Structure
      a. Centralized/decentralized
      b. Departmentalization
      c. New configurations (e.g., hourglass, cluster, network)

(CONTINUED ON NEXT PAGE)

D. Management Skills (20-30%) [Awareness level]
1. Group dynamics
    a. Traits (e.g., cohesiveness, roles, norms, groupthink)
    b. Stages of group development
    c. Organizational politics
    d. Criteria and determinants of effectiveness
2. Team building
    a. Methods used in team building
    b. Assessing team performance
3. Leadership skills
    a. Theories compared and contrasted
    b. Leadership grid (topology of leadership styles)
    c. Mentoring
4. Personal time management

E. Negotiating (5-15%) [Awareness level]
1. Conflict resolution
    a. Competitive/cooperative
    b. Compromise, forcing, smoothing, etc.
2. Added-value negotiating
    a. Description
    b. Specific steps

Format: 125 multiple-choice questions

Certified Internal Auditor (CIA) Model Exam Questions

Part I - The Internal Audit Activity's Role in Governance, Risk, and Control

Part I Model Exam Questions: 100

Questions on actual CIA Exam Part I: 125
(see explanation in "Foreword" on page iii)

Time allowed for completion of CIA Exam Part I: 210 minutes

Instructions such as those that follow will be listed on the cover of each CIA examination. Please read them carefully.

1. Place your candidate number on the answer sheet in the space provided.
2. Do not place extraneous marks on the answer sheet.
3. Be certain that changes to answers are **completely** erased.

4. All references to the *Professional Practices Framework* refer to The IIA's *Professional Practices Framework*, which includes the *Standards* and the *Practice Advisories*. All references to *Standards* refer to the *International Standards for the Professional Practice of Internal Auditing* outlined in The IIA's *Professional Practices Framework*.

Failure to follow these instructions and the "Instructions to Candidates" guidelines could adversely affect both your right to receive the results of this examination and your future participation in the Certified Internal Auditor program.

All papers submitted in completion of any part of this examination become the sole property of The Institute of Internal Auditors, Inc. Candidates may not disclose the contents of this exam unless expressly authorized by the Certification Department.

1. Which of the following is **not** true with regard to the internal audit charter?
   a. It defines the authorities and responsibilities for the internal audit activity.
   b. It specifies the minimum resources needed for the internal audit activity.
   c. It provides a basis for evaluating the internal audit activity.
   d. It should be approved by senior management and the board.

2. Which engagement-planning tool is general in nature and is used to ensure adequate audit coverage over time?
   a. The long-range schedule.
   b. The engagement program.
   c. The audit activity's budget.
   d. The audit activity's charter.

3. The function of internal auditing, as related to internal financial reports, would be to:
   a. Ensure compliance with reporting procedures.
   b. Review the expenditure items and match each item with the expenses incurred.
   c. Determine if there are any employees expending funds without authorization.
   d. Identify inadequate controls that increase the likelihood of unauthorized expenditures.

4. Audit committees are most likely to participate in the approval of:
   a. Audit staff promotions and salary increases.
   b. The internal audit report observations and recommendations.
   c. Audit work schedules.
   d. The appointment of the chief audit executive.

5. According to the *Professional Practices Framework*, the independence of the internal audit activity is achieved through:
   a. Staffing and supervision.
   b. Continuing professional development and due professional care.
   c. Human relations and communications.
   d. Organizational status and objectivity.

6. Which of the following actions would be a violation of auditor independence?
   a. Continuing on an audit assignment at a division for which the auditor will soon be responsible as the result of a promotion.
   b. Reducing the scope of an engagement due to budget restrictions.
   c. Participating on a task force which recommends standards of control for a new distribution system.
   d. Reviewing a purchasing agent's contract drafts prior to their execution.

7. As part of a company-sponsored award program, an internal auditor was offered an award of significant monetary value by a division in recognition of the cost savings that resulted from the auditor's recommendations. According to the *Professional Practices Framework*, what is the most appropriate action for the auditor to take?
   a. Accept the gift since the engagement is already concluded and the report issued.
   b. Accept the award under the condition that any proceeds go to charity.
   c. Inform audit management and ask for direction on whether to accept the gift.
   d. Decline the gift and advise the division manager's superior.

8. In which of the following situations would an auditor potentially lack objectivity?
   a. An auditor reviews the procedures for a new electronic data interchange connection to a major customer before it is implemented.
   b. A former purchasing assistant performs a review of internal controls over purchasing four months after being transferred to the internal audit activity.
   c. An auditor recommends standards of control and performance measures for a contract with a service organization for the processing of payroll and employee benefits.
   d. A payroll accounting employee assists an auditor in verifying the physical inventory of small motors.

9. A CIA, working as the director of purchasing, signs a contract to procure a large order from the supplier with the best price, quality, and performance. Shortly after signing the contract, the supplier presents the CIA with a gift of significant monetary value. Which of the following statements regarding the acceptance of the gift is correct?
   a. Acceptance of the gift would be prohibited only if it were non-customary.
   b. Acceptance of the gift would violate the *IIA Code of Ethics* and would be prohibited for a CIA.
   c. Since the CIA is not acting as an internal auditor, acceptance of the gift would be governed only by the organization's code of conduct.
   d. Since the contract was signed before the gift was offered, acceptance of the gift would not violate either the *IIA Code of Ethics* or the organization's code of conduct.

10. An internal auditor assigned to audit a vendor's compliance with product quality standards is the brother of the vendor's controller. The auditor should:
    a. Accept the assignment, but avoid contact with the controller during fieldwork.
    b. Accept the assignment, but disclose the relationship in the engagement final communication.
    c. Notify the vendor of the potential conflict of interest.
    d. Notify the chief audit executive of the potential conflict of interest.

11. The *Standards* require that internal auditors possess which of the following skills?

    I. Internal auditors should understand human relations and be skilled in dealing with people.
    II. Internal auditors should be able to recognize and evaluate the materiality and significance of deviations from good business practices.
    III. Internal auditors should be experts on subjects such as economics, commercial law, taxation, finance, and information technology.
    IV. Internal auditors should be skilled in oral and written communication.

    a. II only.
    b. I and III only.
    c. III and IV only.
    d. I, II, and IV only.

12. A chief audit executive (CAE) has been requested by the audit committee to conduct an engagement at a chemical factory as soon as possible. The engagement will include reviews of health, safety, and environmental (HSE) management and processes. The CAE knows that the internal audit activity does not possess the HSE knowledge necessary to conduct such an engagement. The CAE should:
    a. Begin the engagement and incorporate HSE training into next year's planning to prepare for a follow-up engagement.
    b. Suggest to the audit committee that the factory's own HSE staff conduct the engagement.
    c. Seek permission from the audit committee to obtain appropriate support from an HSE professional.
    d. Defer the engagement and tell the audit committee that it will take several months to train internal audit staff for such an engagement.

13. To ensure that due professional care has been taken at all times during an engagement, the internal auditor should always:
    a. Ensure that all financial information related to the audit is included in the audit plan and examined for nonconformance or irregularities.
    b. Ensure that all audit tests are fully documented.
    c. Consider the possibility of nonconformance or irregularities at all times during an engagement.
    d. Communicate any noncompliance or irregularity discovered during an engagement promptly to the audit committee.

14. In an assurance engagement of treasury operations, an internal auditor is required to consider all of the following issues **except**:
    a. The audit committee has requested assurance on the treasury department's compliance with a new policy on use of financial instruments.
    b. Treasury management has not instituted any risk management policies.
    c. Due to the recent sale of a division, the amount of cash and marketable securities managed by the treasury department has increased by 350 percent.
    d. The external auditors have indicated some difficulties in obtaining account confirmations.

15. To promote a positive image within an organization, a chief audit executive (CAE) planned to conduct assurance engagements that highlighted potential costs to be saved. Negative observations were to be omitted from engagement final communications. Which action taken by the CAE would be considered a violation of the *Standards*?

    I. The focus of the audit engagements was changed without modifying the charter or consulting the audit committee.
    II. Negative observations were omitted from the engagement final communications.
    III. Cost savings recommendations were highlighted in the engagement final communications.

    a. I only.
    b. I and II only.
    c. I and III only.
    d. II and III only.

16. A chief audit executive (CAE) for a very small internal audit department has just received a request from management to perform an audit of an extremely complex area in which the CAE and the department have no expertise. The nature of the audit engagement is within the scope of internal audit activities. Management has expressed a desire to have the engagement conducted in the very near future because of the high level of risk involved. Which of the following responses by the CAE would be in violation of the *Standards*?
    a. Discuss with management the possibility of outsourcing the audit of this complex area.
    b. Add an outside consultant to the audit staff to assist in the performance of the audit engagement.
    c. Accept the audit engagement and begin immediately, since it is a high-risk area.
    d. Discuss the timeline of the audit engagement with management to determine if sufficient time exists in which to develop appropriate expertise.

17. An auditor, nearly finished with an engagement, discovers that the director of marketing has a gambling habit. The gambling issue is not directly related to the existing engagement and there is pressure to complete the current engagement. The auditor notes the problem and forwards the information to the chief audit executive but performs no further follow-up. The auditor's actions would:
    a. Be in violation of the *IIA Code of Ethics* for withholding meaningful information.
    b. Be in violation of the *Standards* because the auditor did not properly follow up on a red flag that might indicate the existence of fraud.
    c. Not be in violation of either the *IIA Code of Ethics* or *Standards*.
    d. Both a and b.

18. In selecting an instructional strategy for developing internal audit staff, a chief audit executive should begin by reviewing:
    a. Organizational objectives.
    b. Learning content.
    c. Learners' readiness.
    d. Budget constraints.

19. Which of the following activities are designed to provide feedback on the effectiveness of an internal audit function?

    I. Proper supervision.
    II. Proper training.
    III. Internal assessments.
    IV. External assessments.

    a. I, II, and III only.
    b. I, II, and IV only.
    c. I, III, and IV only.
    d. II, III, and IV only.

20. The most important reason for the chief audit executive to ensure that the internal audit department has adequate and sufficient resources is to:
    a. Ensure that the function is adequately protected from outsourcing.
    b. Demonstrate sufficient capability to meet the audit plan requirements.
    c. Establish credibility with the audit committee and management.
    d. Fulfill the need for effective succession planning.

21. Which of the following is part of an internal audit activity's quality assurance program, rather than being included as part of other responsibilities of the chief audit executive (CAE)?
    a. The CAE provides information about and access to internal audit workpapers to the external auditors to enable them to understand and determine the degree to which they may rely on the internal auditors' work.
    b. Management approves a formal charter establishing the purpose, authority, and responsibility of the internal audit activity.
    c. Each individual internal auditor's performance is appraised at least annually.
    d. Supervision of an internal auditor's work is performed throughout each audit engagement.

22. A chief audit executive (CAE) uses a risk assessment model to establish the annual audit plan. Which of the following would be an appropriate action by the CAE?

    I. Maintain ongoing dialogue with management and the audit committee.
    II. Ensure that the schedule of audit priorities remains unchanged.
    III. Employ only quantitative methods to determine risk weightings.
    IV. Revise the risk assessment and audit priorities as warranted.

    a. III only.
    b. I and II only.
    c. I and IV only.
    d. III and IV only.

23. When a risk assessment process has been used to construct an audit engagement schedule, which of the following should receive attention first?
    a. The external auditors have requested assistance for their upcoming annual audit.
    b. A new accounts payable system is currently undergoing testing by the information technology department.
    c. Management has requested an investigation of possible lapping in receivables.
    d. The existing accounts payable system has not been audited over the past year.

24. A chief audit executive is reviewing the following enterprise-wide risk map:

		LIKELIHOOD	
IMPACT		Remote	Possible	Likely
	Critical	Risk A	Risk B	
	Major			Risk D
	Minor		Risk C	

    Which of the following is the correct prioritization of risks, considering limited resources in the internal audit activity?
    a. Risk B, Risk C, Risk A, Risk D.
    b. Risk A, Risk B, Risk C, Risk D.
    c. Risk D, Risk B, Risk C, Risk A.
    d. Risk B, Risk C, Risk D, Risk A.

25. Which of the following represents the best risk assessment technique?
    a. Assessment of the risk levels for future events based on the extent of uncertainty of those events and their impact on achievement of long-term organizational goals.
    b. Assessment of inherent and control risks and their impact on the extent of financial misstatements.
    c. Assessment of the risk levels of current and future events, their effect on achievement of the organization's objectives, and their underlying causes.
    d. Assessment of the risk levels of current and future events, their impact on the organization's mission, and the potential for elimination of existing or possible risk factors.

26. Which of the following is the best reason for the chief audit executive to consider the strategic plan in developing the annual audit plan?
    a. To ensure that the internal audit plan supports the overall business objectives.
    b. To ensure that the internal audit plan will be approved by senior management.
    c. To make recommendations to improve the strategic plan.
    d. To emphasize the importance of the internal audit function.

27. In assessing organizational risk in a manufacturing environment, which of the following would have the most long-range impact on the organization?
    a. Production scheduling.
    b. Inventory policy.
    c. Product quality.
    d. Advertising budget.

28. When assessing the risk associated with an activity, an internal auditor should:
    a. Determine how the risk should best be managed.
    b. Provide assurance on the management of the risk.
    c. Update the risk management process based on risk exposures.
    d. Design controls to mitigate the identified risks.

Use the following information to answer questions 29 through 30.

During the planning phase, a chief audit executive (CAE) is evaluating four audit engagements based on the following factors: the engagement's ability to reduce risk to the organization, the engagement's ability to save the organization money, and the extent of change in the area since the last engagement. The CAE has scored the engagements for each factor from low to high, assigned points, and calculated an overall ranking. The results are shown below with the points in parenthesis:

Audit	Risk Reduction	Cost Savings	Changes
1	High (3)	Medium (2)	Low (1)
2	High (3)	Low (1)	High (3)
3	Low (1)	High (3)	Medium (2)
4	Medium (2)	Medium (2)	High (3)

29. Which audit engagements should the CAE pursue if all factors are weighed equally?
    a. 1 and 2 only.
    b. 1 and 3 only.
    c. 2 and 4 only.
    d. 3 and 4 only.

30. If the organization has asked the CAE to consider the cost savings factor to be twice as important as any other factor, which engagements should the CAE pursue?
    a. 1 and 2 only.
    b. 1 and 3 only.
    c. 2 and 4 only.
    d. 3 and 4 only.

31. If a department outside of the internal audit activity is responsible for reviewing a function or process, the internal auditors should:
    a. Consider the work of the other department when assessing the function or process.
    b. Ignore the work of the other department and proceed with an independent audit.
    c. Reduce the scope of the audit since the work has already been performed by the other department.
    d. Yield the responsibility for assessing the function or process to the other department.

32. Who has primary responsibility for providing information to the audit committee on the professional and organizational benefits of coordinating internal audit assurance and consulting activities with other assurance and consulting activities?
    a. The external auditor.
    b. The chief audit executive.
    c. The chief executive officer.
    d. Each assurance and consulting function.

33. Using the internal audit department to coordinate regulatory examiners' efforts is beneficial to the organization because internal auditors can:
    a. Influence the regulatory examiners' interpretation of law to match corporate practice.
    b. Recommend changes in scope to limit bias by the regulatory examiners.
    c. Perform fieldwork for the regulatory examiners and thus reduce the amount of time regulatory examiners are on-site.
    d. Supply evidence of adequate compliance testing through internal audit workpapers and reports.

34. A chief audit executive would most likely use risk assessment for audit planning because it provides:
    a. A systematic process for assessing and integrating professional judgment about probable adverse conditions.
    b. A listing of potentially adverse effects on the organization.
    c. A list of auditable activities in the organization.
    d. The probability that an event or action may adversely affect the organization.

35. In deciding whether to schedule the purchasing or the personnel department for an audit engagement, which of the following would be the **least** important factor?
    a. There have been major changes in operations in one of the departments.
    b. The audit staff has recently added an individual with expertise in one of the areas.
    c. There are more opportunities to achieve operating benefits in one of the departments than in the other.
    d. The potential for loss is significantly greater in one department than in the other.

36. The internal audit activity of a large corporation has established its operating plan and budget for the coming year. The operating plan is restricted to the following categories: a prioritized listing of all engagements, staffing, a detailed expense budget, and the commencement date of each engagement. Which of the following best describes the major deficiency of this operating plan?
    a. Requests by management for special projects are not considered.
    b. Opportunities to achieve operating benefits are ignored.
    c. Measurability criteria and targeted dates of completion are not provided.
    d. Knowledge, skills, and disciplines required to perform work are ignored.

37. To improve audit efficiency, internal auditors can rely upon the work of external auditors that is:
    a. Performed after the internal audit engagement.
    b. Primarily concerned with operational objectives and activities.
    c. Coordinated with internal audit activity.
    d. Conducted in accordance with the *IIA Code of Ethics*.

38. The internal audit activity has recently experienced the departure of two internal auditors who cannot be immediately replaced due to budget constraints. Which of the following is the **least** desirable option for efficiently completing future engagements, given this reduction in resources?
    a. Using self-assessment questionnaires to address audit objectives.
    b. Employing information technology in audit planning, sampling, and documentation.
    c. Eliminating consulting engagements from the engagement work schedule.
    d. Filling vacancies with personnel from operating departments that are not being audited.

39. If the annual audit plan does not allow for adequate review of compliance with all material regulations affecting the company, the internal audit activity should:
    a. Ensure that the board of directors and senior management are aware of the limitation.
    b. Include a memo with the audit planning file listing the reasons for the lack of coverage.
    c. Document that regulations not included will be reviewed in the subsequent year.
    d. Decrease the scope of operational and financial audits to make additional audit time available.

40. Which of the following comments is correct regarding the assessment of risk associated with two projects that are competing for limited audit resources?

    I. Activities that are requested by the audit committee should always be considered higher risk than those requested by management.
    II. Activities with higher dollar budgets should always be considered higher risk than those with lower dollar budgets.
    III. Risk should always be measured by the potential dollar or adverse exposure to the organization.

    a. I only.
    b. II only.
    c. III only.
    d. I and III only.

41. Which of the following activities undertaken by the internal auditor might be in conflict with the standard of independence?
    a. Risk management consultant.
    b. Product development team leader.
    c. Ethics advocate.
    d. External audit liaison.

42. The internal audit activity should contribute to the organization's governance process by evaluating the processes through which:

    I. Ethics and values are promoted.
    II. Effective organizational performance management and accountability are ensured.
    III. Risk and control information is communicated.
    IV. Activities of the external and internal auditors and management are coordinated.

    a. I only.
    b. IV only.
    c. II and III only.
    d. I, II, III, and IV.

43. In a well-developed management environment, the internal audit activity would:
    a. Report the results of an audit engagement to line management as well as to senior management.
    b. Conduct initial audits of new computer systems after they have begun operating.
    c. Interface primarily with senior management, minimizing interactions with line managers who are the subjects of internal audit work.
    d. Focus primarily on asset management and report results to the audit committee.

44. Which of the following best describes an internal auditor's purpose in reviewing the organization's existing risk management, control, and governance processes?
    a. To help determine the nature, timing, and extent of tests necessary to achieve engagement objectives.
    b. To ensure that weaknesses in the internal control system are corrected.
    c. To provide reasonable assurance that the processes will enable the organization's objectives and goals to be met efficiently and economically.
    d. To determine whether the processes ensure that the accounting records are correct and that financial statements are fairly stated.

45. Which of the following represents the best governance structure?

	Operating Management	Executive Management	Internal Auditing
a.	Responsibility for risk	Oversight role	Advisory role
b.	Oversight role	Responsibility for risk	Advisory role
c.	Responsibility for risk	Advisory role	Oversight role
d.	Oversight role	Advisory role	Responsibility for risk

46. Which of the following is **not** a responsibility of the chief audit executive?
    a. To communicate the internal audit activity's plans and resource requirements to senior management and the board for review and approval.
    b. To coordinate with other internal and external providers of audit and consulting services to ensure proper coverage and minimize duplication.
    c. To oversee the establishment, administration, and assessment of the organization's system of risk management processes.
    d. To follow up on whether appropriate management actions have been taken on significant reported risks.

47. Which statement most accurately describes how criteria are established for use by internal auditors in determining whether goals and objectives have been accomplished?
    a. Management is responsible for establishing the criteria.
    b. Internal auditors should use professional standards or government regulations to establish the criteria.
    c. The industry in which a company operates establishes criteria for each member company through benchmarks and best practices for that industry.
    d. Appropriate accounting or auditing standards, including international standards, should be used as the criteria.

48. Which of the following is **not** a role of the internal audit activity in best practice governance activities?
    a. Support the board in enterprise-wide risk assessment.
    b. Ensure the timely implementation of audit recommendations.
    c. Monitor compliance with the corporate code of conduct.
    d. Discuss areas of significant risks.

49. Assessments of the independence of an organization's external auditors should:
    a. Be carried out only when the external auditor is appointed.
    b. Not include any participation by the internal audit activity.
    c. Include the internal audit activity only when the external auditor is appointed.
    d. Include the internal audit activity at the time of appointment and regularly thereafter.

50. During a review of contracts, a chief audit executive (CAE) suspects that a supplier was given an unfair advantage in bidding on a contract. After learning that the chief executive officer (CEO) of the company is a member of the supplier's board of directors, how should the CAE proceed?
    a. Submit a draft report to senior management, excluding the CEO.
    b. Contact the organization's external auditors for assistance.
    c. Obtain supporting documentation and present the finding to the chairperson of the audit committee.
    d. Immediately notify the board of directors.

51. Company A has a formal corporate code of ethics while company B does not. The code of ethics covers such things as purchase agreements and relationships with vendors as well as many other issues to guide individual behavior within the company. Which of the following statements can be logically inferred?

    I. Company A exhibits a higher standard of ethical behavior than does company B.
    II. Company A has established objective criteria by which an employee's actions can be evaluated.
    III. The absence of a formal corporate code of ethics in company B would prevent a successful audit of ethical behavior in that company.

    a. II only.
    b. III only.
    c. I and II only.
    d. II and III only.

52. Management and the board of directors are responsible for following up on observations and recommendations made by the external auditors. What role, if any, should the internal audit activity have in this process?
    a. The internal audit activity should have no role in this process in order to ensure independence.
    b. The internal audit activity should only become involved if the chief audit executive has sufficient evidence that the follow-up is not occurring.
    c. The internal audit activity should establish a monitoring process to review the adequacy and effectiveness of management's follow-up actions.
    d. The internal audit activity should become involved only if specifically requested by management or the board of directors.

53. The primary reason that a bank would maintain a separate compliance function is to:
    a. Better manage perceived high risks.
    b. Strengthen controls over the bank's investments.
    c. Ensure the independence of line and senior management.
    d. Better respond to shareholder expectations.

54. The function of the chief risk officer (CRO) is most effective when the CRO:
    a. Manages risk as a member of senior management.
    b. Shares the management of risk with line management.
    c. Shares the management of risk with the chief audit executive.
    d. Monitors risk as part of the enterprise risk management team.

55. To minimize potential financial losses associated with physical assets, the assets should be insured in an amount that is:
    a. Supported by periodic appraisals.
    b. Determined by the board of directors.
    c. Automatically adjusted by an economic indicator such as the consumer price index.
    d. Equal to the book value of the individual assets.

56. Which of the following statements is correct regarding corporate compensation systems and related bonuses?

   I. A bonus system should be considered part of the control environment of an organization and should be considered in formulating a report on internal control.
   II. Compensation systems are not part of an organization's control system and should not be reported as such.
   III. An audit of an organization's compensation system should be performed independently of an audit of the control system over other functions that impact corporate bonuses.

   a. I only.
   b. II only.
   c. III only.
   d. II and III only.

57. Which of the following statements regarding corporate governance is **not** correct?
   a. Corporate control mechanisms include internal and external mechanisms.
   b. The compensation scheme for management is part of the corporate control mechanisms.
   c. The dilution of shareholders' wealth resulting from employee stock options or employee stock bonuses is an accounting issue rather than a corporate governance issue.
   d. The internal auditor of a company has more responsibility than the board for the company's corporate governance.

58. The activity of trading futures with the objective of reducing or controlling risk is called:
   a. Insuring.
   b. Hedging.
   c. Short-selling.
   d. Factoring.

59. Enterprise risk management:
   a. Guarantees achievement of organizational objectives.
   b. Requires establishment of risk and control activities by internal auditors.
   c. Involves the identification of events with negative impacts on organizational objectives.
   d. Includes selection of the best risk response for the organization.

60. What is residual risk?
   a. Impact of risk.
   b. Risk that is under control.
   c. Risk that is not managed.
   d. Underlying risk in the environment.

Use the following information to answer questions 61 through 62.

The marketing department for a major retailer assigns separate product managers for each product line. Product managers are responsible for ordering products and determining retail pricing. Each product manager's purchasing budget is set by the marketing manager. Products are delivered to a central distribution center where goods are segregated for distribution to the company's 52 department stores. Because receipts are recorded at the distribution center, the company does not maintain a receiving function at each store. Product managers are evaluated on a combination of sales and gross profit generated from their product lines. Many products are seasonal and individual store managers can require that seasonal products be removed to make space for the next season's products.

61. Which of the following is a control deficiency in this situation?
   a. The store manager can require items to be removed, thus affecting the potential performance evaluation of individual product managers.
   b. The product manager negotiates the purchase price and sets the selling price.
   c. Evaluating product managers by total gross profit generated by product line will lead to dysfunctional behavior.
   d. There is no receiving function located at individual stores.

62. Requests for purchases beyond those initially budgeted must be approved by the marketing manager. This procedure:

   I. Should provide for the most efficient allocation of scarce organizational resources.
   II. Is a detective control procedure.
   III. Is unnecessary because each product manager is evaluated on profit generated.

   a. I only.
   b. III only.
   c. II and III only.
   d. I, II, and III.

63. An organization's management perceives the need to make significant changes. Which of the following factors is management **least** likely to be able to change?
   a. The organization's members.
   b. The organization's structure.
   c. The organization's environment.
   d. The organization's technology.

64. Many organizations use electronic funds transfer to pay their suppliers instead of issuing checks. Regarding the risks associated with issuing checks, which of the following risk management techniques does this represent?
   a. Controlling.
   b. Accepting.
   c. Transferring.
   d. Avoiding.

65. Which of the following goals sets risk management strategies at the optimum level?
   a. Minimize costs.
   b. Maximize market share.
   c. Minimize losses.
   d. Maximize shareholder value.

66. Of the following reasons for employees to resist a major change in organizational processes, which is **least** likely?
   a. Threat of loss of jobs.
   b. Required attendance at training classes.
   c. Breakup of existing work groups.
   d. Imposition of new processes by senior management without prior discussion.

67. All of the following would be part of a factory's control system to prevent release of waste water that does not meet discharge standards **except**:
   a. Performing chemical analysis of the water, prior to discharge, for components specified in the permit.
   b. Specifying (by policy, training, and advisory signs) which substances may be disposed of via sinks and floor drains within the factory.
   c. Periodically flushing sinks and floor drains with a large volume of clean water to ensure pollutants are sufficiently diluted.
   d. Establishing a preventive maintenance program for the factory's pretreatment system.

68. An organization is changing to a quality assurance program that incorporates quality throughout the process. This is very different from its years of dependence on quality control at the end of the process. This type of change is a:
   a. Cultural change.
   b. Product change.
   c. Structural change.
   d. Organizational change.

69. A chief audit executive plans to make changes that may be perceived negatively by the audit staff. The best way to reduce resistance would be to:
   a. Develop the new approach fully before presenting it to the audit staff.
   b. Ask the chief executive officer (CEO) to approve the changes and have the CEO attend the departmental staff meeting when they are presented.
   c. Approach the staff with the general idea and involve them in the development of the changes.
   d. Get the internal audit activity's clients to support the changes.

70. During a meeting of an internal audit project team, two members of the team disagree, and one accuses the other of trying to advance personal interests over the interests of the audit. The audit manager should:
   a. Discipline both auditors after the meeting for their lack of professional conduct.
   b. Continue the meeting but speak to the accusing auditor later regarding the inappropriate conduct.
   c. Meet with both auditors after the meeting to resolve the conflict and the inappropriate behavior.
   d. Stop the meeting and refer the matter to the entire team for discussion.

71. The control that would most likely ensure that payroll checks are written only for authorized amounts is to:
   a. Conduct periodic floor verification of employees on the payroll.
   b. Require the return of undelivered checks to the cashier.
   c. Require supervisory approval of employee time cards.
   d. Periodically witness the distribution of payroll checks.

72. Which of the following controls would prevent the ordering of quantities in excess of an organization's needs?
    a. Review of all purchase requisitions by a supervisor in the user department prior to submitting them to the purchasing department.
    b. Automatic reorder by the purchasing department when low inventory level is indicated by the system.
    c. A policy requiring review of the purchase order before receiving a new shipment.
    d. A policy requiring agreement of the receiving report and packing slip before storage of new receipts.

73. Which of the following observations by an auditor is most likely to indicate the existence of control weaknesses over safeguarding of assets?

    I.   A service department's location is not well suited to allow adequate service to other units.
    II. Employees hired for sensitive positions are not subjected to background checks.
    III. Managers do not have access to reports that profile overall performance in relation to other benchmarked organizations.
    IV. Management has not taken corrective action to resolve past engagement observations related to inventory controls.

    a. I and II only.
    b. I and IV only.
    c. II and III only.
    d. II and IV only.

74. A control likely to prevent purchasing agents from favoring specific suppliers is:
    a. Requiring management's review of a monthly report of the totals spent by each buyer.
    b. Requiring buyers to adhere to detailed material specifications.
    c. Rotating buyer assignments periodically.
    d. Monitoring the number of orders placed by each buyer.

75. Which of the following would minimize defects in finished goods caused by poor quality raw materials?
    a. Documented procedures for the proper handling of work-in-process inventory.
    b. Required material specifications for all purchases.
    c. Timely follow-up on all unfavorable usage variances.
    d. Determination of the amount of spoilage at the end of the manufacturing process.

76. The requirement that purchases be made from suppliers on an approved vendor list is an example of a:
    a. Preventive control.
    b. Detective control.
    c. Corrective control.
    d. Monitoring control.

77. Appropriate internal control for a multinational corporation's branch office that has a monetary transfer unit requires that:
    a. The individual who initiates wire transfers not reconcile the bank statement.
    b. The branch manager receive all wire transfers.
    c. Foreign currency rates be computed separately by two different employees.
    d. Corporate management approve the hiring of monetary transfer unit employees.

78. Which of the following best describes a preliminary survey?
    a. A standardized questionnaire used to obtain an understanding of management objectives.
    b. A statistical sample to review key employee attitudes, skills, and knowledge.
    c. A walk-through of the financial control system to identify risks and the controls that can address those risks.
    d. A process used to become familiar with activities and risks in order to identify areas for engagement emphasis.

79. During a preliminary survey, an auditor found that several accounts payable vouchers for major suppliers required adjustments for duplicate payment of prior invoices. This would indicate:
    a. A need for additional testing to determine related controls and the current exposure to duplicate payments made to suppliers.
    b. The possibility of unrecorded liabilities for the amount of the overpayments.
    c. Insufficient controls in the receiving area to ensure timely notice to the accounts payable area that goods have been received and inspected.
    d. The existence of a sophisticated accounts payable system that correlates overpayments to open invoices and therefore requires no further audit concern.

I - 12

80. Which of the following procedures should be performed as part of a preliminary review in an audit of a bank's investing and lending activities?
    a. Review reports of audits performed by regulatory and outside auditors since the last internal audit engagement.
    b. Interview management to identify changes made in policies regarding investments or loans.
    c. Review minutes of the board of directors' meetings to identify changes in policies affecting investments and loans.
    d. All of the above.

81. During an assessment of the risk associated with sales contracts and related commissions, which of the following factors would most likely result in an expansion of the engagement scope?
    a. An increase in product sales, along with an increase in commissions.
    b. An increase in sales returns, along with an increase in commissions.
    c. A decrease in sales commissions, along with a decrease in product sales.
    d. A decrease in sales returns, along with an increase in product sales.

82. An auditor, experienced in air-quality issues, discovered a significant lack of knowledge about legal requirements for controlling air emissions while interviewing the manager of the environmental, health, and safety (EHS) department. The auditor should:
    a. Alter the scope of the engagement to focus on activities associated with air emissions.
    b. Share extensive personal knowledge with the EHS manager.
    c. Take note of the weakness and direct additional questions to determine the potential effect of the lack of knowledge.
    d. Report potential violations in this area to the appropriate regulatory agency.

83. Which of the following is an appropriate statement of an audit engagement objective?
    a. To observe the physical inventory count.
    b. To determine whether inventory stocks are sufficient to meet projected sales.
    c. To search for the existence of obsolete inventory by computing inventory turnover by product line.
    d. To include information about stockouts in the engagement final communication.

84. An internal auditor plans to conduct an audit of the adequacy of controls over investments in new financial instruments. Which of the following would **not** be required as part of such an engagement?
    a. Determine if policies exist which describe the risks the treasurer may take and the types of instruments in which the treasurer may make investments.
    b. Determine the extent of management oversight over investments in sophisticated instruments.
    c. Determine whether the treasurer is getting higher or lower rates of return on investments than are treasurers in comparable organizations.
    d. Determine the nature of controls established by the treasurer to monitor the risks in the investments.

85. If a department's operating standards are vague and thus subject to interpretation, an auditor should:
    a. Seek agreement with the departmental manager as to the criteria needed to measure operating performance.
    b. Determine best practices in the area and use them as the standard.
    c. Interpret the standards in their strictest sense because standards are otherwise only minimum measures of acceptance.
    d. Omit any comments on standards and the department's performance in relationship to those standards, because such an analysis would be inappropriate.

86. If an auditor's preliminary evaluation of internal controls results in an observation that controls may be inadequate, the next step would be to:
    a. Expand audit work prior to the preparation of an engagement final communication.
    b. Prepare a flowchart depicting the internal control system.
    c. Note an exception in the engagement final communication if losses have occurred.
    d. Implement the desired controls.

Use the following information to answer questions 87 through 88.

The manager of a production line has the authority to order and receive replacement parts for all machinery that require periodic maintenance. The internal auditor received an anonymous tip that the manager ordered substantially more parts than were necessary from a family member in the parts supply business. The unneeded parts were never delivered. Instead, the manager processed receiving documents and charged the parts to machinery maintenance accounts. The payments for the undelivered parts were sent to the supplier, and the money was divided between the manager and the family member.

87. Which of the following internal controls would have most likely prevented this fraud from occurring?
    a. Establishing predefined spending levels for all vendors during the bidding process.
    b. Segregating the receiving function from the authorization of parts purchases.
    c. Comparing the bill of lading for replacement parts to the approved purchase order.
    d. Using the company's inventory system to match quantities requested with quantities received.

88. Which of the following tests would best assist the auditor in deciding whether to investigate this anonymous tip further?
    a. Comparison of the current quarter's maintenance expense with prior-period activity.
    b. Physical inventory testing of replacement parts for existence and valuation.
    c. Analysis of repair parts charged to maintenance to review the reasonableness of the number of items replaced.
    d. Review of a test sample of parts invoices for proper authorization and receipt.

89. When faced with an imposed scope limitation, a chief audit executive should:
    a. Delay the engagement until the scope limitation is removed.
    b. Communicate the potential effects of the scope limitation to the audit committee of the board of directors.
    c. Increase the frequency of auditing the activity in question.
    d. Assign more experienced personnel to the engagement.

90. An auditor has been assigned to analyze the effectiveness of a set of rehabilitation programs. The programs have been in operation for ten years and have not been evaluated. The organization providing the program data asserts that the data are incomplete. The auditor should:
    a. Perform the analysis anyway, assessing the effects of the incomplete data, but disclaim any assertion regarding data reliability.
    b. Trace a randomly chosen set of records to source files to assess the accuracy and completeness of the data provided.
    c. Not perform the analysis.
    d. Postpone the analysis until data are complete.

91. Which of the following fraudulent entries is most likely to be made to conceal the theft of an asset?
    a. Debit expenses, and credit the asset.
    b. Debit the asset, and credit another asset account.
    c. Debit revenue, and credit the asset.
    d. Debit another asset account, and credit the asset.

92. An adequate system of internal controls is most likely to detect an irregularity perpetrated by a:
    a. Group of employees in collusion.
    b. Single employee.
    c. Group of managers in collusion.
    d. Single manager.

93. Divisional management stated that a recent gross margin increase was due to increased efficiency in manufacturing operations. Which of the following audit procedures would be most relevant to that assertion?
    a. Obtain a physical count of inventory.
    b. Select a sample of products, then compare costs-per-unit this year to those of last year, test cost buildups, and analyze standard cost variances.
    c. Take a physical inventory of equipment to determine if there were significant changes.
    d. Select a sample of finished goods inventory and trace raw materials cost back to purchase prices in order to determine the accuracy of the recorded raw materials price.

Use the following information to answer questions 94 through 95.

A company maintains production data on personal computers, connected by a local area network (LAN), and uses the data to generate automatic purchases via electronic data interchange. Purchases are made from authorized vendors based on production plans for the next month and on an authorized materials requirements plan (MRP) which identifies the parts needed for each unit of production.

94. The production line has experienced shutdowns because needed production parts were not on hand. Which of the following audit procedures would best identify the cause of the parts shortages?
    a. Determine if access controls are sufficient to restrict the input of incorrect data into the production database.
    b. Use generalized audit software to develop a complete list of the parts shortages that caused each of the production shutdowns, and analyze this data.
    c. Select a random sample of parts on hand per the personal computer databases and compare with actual parts on hand.
    d. Select a random sample of production information for selected days and trace input into the production database maintained on the LAN.

95. Which of the following audit procedures would be most effective in determining if purchasing requirements have been updated for changes in production techniques?
    a. Recalculate parts needed based on current production estimates and the MRP for the revised production techniques. Compare these needs with purchase orders generated from the system for the same period.
    b. Develop test data to input into the LAN and compare purchase orders generated from test data with purchase orders generated from production data.
    c. Use generalized audit software to develop a report of excess inventory. Compare the inventory with current production volume.
    d. Select a sample of production estimates and MRPs for several periods and trace them into the system to determine that input is accurate.

96. Which of the following factors would be considered the **least** important in deciding whether existing internal audit resources should be moved from an ongoing compliance audit engagement to a division audit engagement requested by management?
    a. A financial audit of the division performed by the external auditor a year ago.
    b. The potential for fraud associated with the ongoing engagement.
    c. An increase in the level of expenditures experienced by the division for the past year.
    d. The potential for significant regulatory fines associated with the ongoing engagement.

97. As a means of controlling projects and avoiding time-budget overruns, decisions to revise time budgets for an audit engagement should normally be made:
    a. Immediately after completing the preliminary survey.
    b. When a significant deficiency has been substantiated.
    c. When inexperienced audit staff members are assigned to an engagement.
    d. Immediately after expanding tests to establish reliability of observations.

98. Determining that engagement objectives have been met is ultimately the responsibility of the:
    a. Internal auditor.
    b. Audit committee.
    c. Internal audit supervisor.
    d. Chief audit executive.

99. A standardized internal audit engagement program would **not** be appropriate for which of the following situations?
    a. A stable operating environment undergoing only minimal changes.
    b. A complex or changing operating environment.
    c. Multiple branches with similar operations.
    d. Subsequent inventory audit engagements performed at the same location.

100. Audit engagement programs testing internal controls should:
   a. Be tailored for the audit of each operation.
   b. Be generalized to fit all situations without regard to departmental lines.
   c. Be generalized so as to be usable at various international locations of an organization.
   d. Reduce costly duplication of effort by ensuring that every aspect of an operation is examined.

END OF PART I QUESTIONS

PLEASE NOTE: The actual CIA exam Part I will contain *125 exam questions*. The 125 questions will include up to 25 unscored questions, which will be used for research purposes. These unscored questions will be interspersed with the scored questions and will not be identified as unscored questions. Candidates should therefore answer all 125 questions to the best of their ability.

Solutions for Part I – The Internal Audit Activity's Role in Governance, Risk, and Control

The solutions and suggested explanations for Part I of the Certified Internal Auditor Model Exam Questions are provided on the following pages.

The chart below cross-references the question numbers for Part I with the topics tested:

Topic Tested	Question Number
Comply with The IIA's Attribute Standards	1 – 21
Establish a Risk-based Plan to Determine the Priorities of the Internal Audit Activity	22 – 40
Understand the Internal Audit Activity's Role in Organizational Governance	41 – 52
Perform other Internal Audit Roles and Responsibilities	53 – 55
Governance, Risk, and Control Knowledge Elements	56 – 77
Plan Engagements	78 – 100

1. **Solution: b**
   a. Incorrect. The internal audit charter defines the necessary authorities and responsibilities.
   b. Correct. The internal audit manual and annual audit plan help in determining the resource requirements.
   c. Incorrect. The internal audit charter defines the role and responsibility of the internal audit activity and acts as a benchmark for evaluating the audit function.
   d. Incorrect. The internal audit charter should be approved by senior management and by the board.

2. **Solution: a**
   a. Correct. The long-range schedule provides evidence of coverage of key functions at planned intervals.
   b. Incorrect. The engagement program is limited in scope to a particular project.
   c. Incorrect. The audit activity's budget may be used to justify the number of audit personnel, but it is not used to ensure adequate audit coverage over time.
   d. Incorrect. The audit activity's charter is not an engagement-planning tool.

3. **Solution: d**
   a. Incorrect. The *Standards* do not require internal auditors to ensure compliance with reporting procedures.
   b. Incorrect. There is no expected match of funds flows with expense items in a single time period.
   c. Incorrect. This would be a function of the personnel and/or finance departments.
   d. Correct. Internal auditors are responsible for identifying inadequate controls, for appraising managerial effectiveness, and for pinpointing common risks.

4. **Solution: d**
   a. Incorrect. The company's chief audit executive is responsible for staff promotions.
   b. Incorrect. The company's chief audit executive is responsible for approving internal audit reports.
   c. Incorrect. This is a part of the internal audit activity's planning function.
   d. Correct. The independence of the internal audit activity is enhanced when the audit committee participates in naming the chief audit executive.

5. **Solution: d**
   a. Incorrect. Staffing and supervision relate to the professional proficiency of the internal audit activity.
   b. Incorrect. Continuing professional development and due professional care relate to the professional proficiency of the internal auditor.
   c. Incorrect. Human relations and communications relate to the professional proficiency of the internal auditor.
   d. Correct. According to Practice Advisory 1100-1.1, organizational status and objectivity permit members of the internal audit activity to render the impartial and unbiased judgments essential to the proper conduct of engagements.

6. **Solution: a**
   a. Correct. An auditor who has been promoted to an operating department should not continue on an audit of that department. According to Practice Advisory 1130-1.1, the chief audit executive should reassign auditors if a conflict of interest or bias may be reasonably inferred.
   b. Incorrect. Budget restrictions do not constitute a violation of an auditor's independence.
   c. Incorrect. Practice Advisory 1130.A1-1.4 states that an auditor may recommend standards of control for new systems. However, designing, installing, or operating such systems might impair objectivity.
   d. Incorrect. An auditor may review contracts prior to their execution.

7. **Solution: c**
   a. Incorrect. Audit management should always be informed concerning any such offers.
   b. Incorrect. Audit management should always be informed concerning any such offers.
   c. Correct. Audit management should be consulted for guidance.
   d. Incorrect. This could erode the audit function's relationship with the division in question. Audit management should first be informed and consulted for guidance.

8. **Solution: b**
   a. Incorrect. Practice Advisory 1130.A1-1.4 states that the internal auditor's objectivity is not adversely affected when the auditor reviews procedures before they are implemented.
   b. Correct. Practice Advisory 1130.A1-1.3 states that persons transferred to the internal audit activity should not be assigned to audit those activities that they previously performed until a reasonable period of time (at least one year) has elapsed.
   c. Incorrect. Practice Advisory 1130.A1-1.4 states that the internal auditor's objectivity is not adversely affected when the auditor recommends standards of control for systems before they are implemented.
   d. Incorrect. Use of staff from other areas to assist the internal auditor does not impair objectivity, especially when the staff is from outside the area being audited.

9. **Solution: b**
   a. Incorrect. Acceptance of the gift could easily be presumed to have impaired independence and thus would not be acceptable.
   b. Correct. As long as an individual is a Certified Internal Auditor, he or she should be guided by the profession's *Code of Ethics* in addition to the organization's code of conduct. Rule of Conduct 2.2 of the *IIA Code of Ethics* would preclude such a gift because it could be presumed to have influenced the individual's decision.
   c. Incorrect. See answer "b".
   d. Incorrect. See answer "b". Further, there is not sufficient information given to judge possible violations of the organization's code of conduct. However, the action could easily be perceived as a kickback.

10. **Solution: d**
    a. Incorrect. Even if the auditor avoided contact with the controller, there would still be the appearance of conflict of interest.
    b. Incorrect. Situations of potential conflict of interest or bias should be avoided, not merely disclosed.
    c. Incorrect. Conflicts of interest should be reported to the chief audit executive, not the vendor or engagement client.
    d. Correct. Practice Advisory 1130-1.1 states that internal auditors should report to the chief audit executive any situations in which a conflict of interest or bias is present or may reasonably be inferred.

11. **Solution: d (I, II, and IV only)**
    I, II, IV. Correct. Internal auditors are expected to be able to recognize good business practices, understand human relations, and be skilled in oral and written communications.
    III. Incorrect. Internal auditors are not expected to be experts in a wide variety of fields related to their audit responsibilities.

12. **Solution: c**
    a. Incorrect. The chief audit executive (CAE) should not begin the audit without notifying the audit committee of the knowledge issue and attempting to resolve it.
    b. Incorrect. This would not provide the audit committee with an independent review of the HSE management and processes.
    c. Correct. When a CAE recognizes that the internal audit activity does not possess the necessary knowledge and skills for a planned or requested engagement, the audit committee should be requested to approve the use of appropriate independent resources, according to Practice Advisory 1210.A1-1.1.
    d. Incorrect. This delay may have serious consequences because of the nature of the HSE issues involved.

13. **Solution: c**
    a. Incorrect. The automatic inclusion of financial information in an audit does not guarantee that due professional care has been achieved for the audit as a whole.
    b. Incorrect. Keeping detailed working papers does not ensure that due professional care has been taken during the tests.
    c. Correct. Considering the possibility of nonconformance or material irregularities at all times during an engagement is the only way of demonstrating that due professional care has been taken in an internal audit assignment, according to Practice Advisory 1220-1.2.
    d. Incorrect. Due professional care does not require that all instances of noncompliance or irregularity be reported to the audit committee.

14. **Solution: d**
    a. Incorrect. Standard 1220.A1 states that the auditor should consider the extent of work needed to achieve the engagement's objectives. This is a specific engagement objective.
    b. Incorrect. Standard 1220.A1 states that the auditor should consider the adequacy and effectiveness of risk management processes.
    c. Incorrect. Standard 1220.A1 states that the auditor should consider significance and materiality of matters to which assurance procedures are applied. This is a significant increase.
    d. Correct. This is the responsibility of the external auditors and should not change what should be considered by the internal auditor.

15. **Solution: b (I and II only)**
    I, II. Correct. The chief audit executive (CAE) dramatically changed the nature of the audit function without consulting the audit committee or modifying the internal audit charter. Attribute Standard 1000 states that the purpose, authority, and responsibility of the internal audit activity should be formally defined in a charter, consistent with the *Standards*, and approved by the board. Performance Standard 2400 requires that internal auditors communicate the engagement results. Performance Standard 2420 states that communications should be accurate, objective, clear, concise, constructive, complete, and timely. Practice Advisory 2420-1 states that complete communications are lacking nothing that is essential to the target audience and include all significant and relevant information and observations to support recommendations and conclusions.
    III. Incorrect. Highlighting potential cost savings is appropriate for an engagement final communication.

16. **Solution: c**
    a. Incorrect. Outsourcing would be an appropriate response when auditors do not possess the needed background or skills and cannot develop such skills in a timely fashion.
    b. Incorrect. Adding a consultant would be an appropriate response when auditors do not possess the needed background or skills and cannot develop such skills in a timely fashion.
    c. Correct. Planning and executing the audit engagement without the appropriate background and skills would be in violation of Attribute Standard 1210. Attribute Standard 1210 requires that the internal audit department provide assurance that the technical proficiency and educational background of internal auditors are appropriate for the audits to be performed. The auditors do not have such expertise.
    d. Incorrect. Determining whether there is sufficient time and ability to develop such skills would be an appropriate response. Internal auditors should be committed to life-long learning, and thus it would not be unreasonable to have them expand their knowledge and skill set.

17. **Solution: c**
    a. Incorrect. The auditor is not withholding information because the information has been forwarded to the chief audit executive. The information may be useful in a subsequent engagement in the marketing area.
    b. Incorrect. The auditor has documented a red flag that may be important in a subsequent engagement. This does not violate the *Standards*.
    c. Correct. There is no violation of either the *Code of Ethics* or the *Standards*. See answers "a" and "b".
    d. Incorrect. See answers "a" and "b".

18. **Solution: a**
    a. Correct. Without objectives, there is no direction to achieve the strategy.
    b. Incorrect. Without objective setting, content cannot be outlined.
    c. Incorrect. Learners' readiness should be considered after determining objectives.
    d. Incorrect. Budget constraints should be considered later in the process.

19. **Solution: c (I, III, and IV only)**
    I. Correct. Quality assurance programs are designed to provide feedback on the effectiveness of an internal audit function. A quality assurance program should include supervision, which provides day-to-day feedback.
    II. Incorrect. Proper training is important but it does not provide feedback.
    III. Correct. A quality assurance program should include internal assessments.
    IV. Correct. A quality assurance program should include external assessments.

20. **Solution: b**
    a. Incorrect. The decision to outsource the internal audit function is not primarily based on existing resources.
    b. Correct. Standard 2030 requires that resources be adequate and sufficient.
    c. Incorrect. The amount of resources is not a significant factor in establishing credibility.
    d. Incorrect. Succession planning is not related to the amount of audit resources.

21. **Solution: d**
    a. Incorrect. This statement relates to the responsibility of the chief audit executive (CAE) to coordinate with external auditors (Performance Standard 2050 and related Practice Advisory 2050-1).
    b. Incorrect. A CAE's responsibility to seek approval of a charter which establishes authority, purpose, and responsibility (Attribute Standard 1000 and related Practice Advisory 1000-1) is not part of a quality assurance program.
    c. Incorrect. Individual performance appraisals are part of a CAE's responsibility toward personnel management and development (Performance Standard 2030 and related Practice Advisory 2030-1).
    d. Correct. Supervision is one method of ongoing review, which is part of the internal assessment aspect of quality assurance (Practice Advisory 1311-1.1).

22. **Solution: c (I and IV only)**
    I, IV. Correct. It is a best practice for risk assessment to be a dynamic process, changing over time and as new information, business strategies, and risks are identified. Ongoing consultation with members of management and the audit committee is a way for the internal audit activity to obtain such information and stay attuned to organizational developments that may impact existing audit priorities. In order to accommodate such emerging priorities, the work schedule may need to be altered.
    II. Incorrect. Audit schedules will likely change regularly to meet the needs of the organization, particularly if based on an effective risk assessment process.
    III. Incorrect. The weighting of risk is both a quantitative and a qualitative (judgment) exercise.

23. **Solution: c**
    a. Incorrect. External audit requests to assist with fieldwork should be subordinate to fraud investigations.
    b. Incorrect. Since the new system is not yet in production, this can wait.
    c. Correct. Management's request to investigate a possible fraud in the accounts receivable unit must take precedence over the other entities.
    d. Incorrect. A management request involving a fraud should take priority over a system that has not been audited over the past year.

24. **Solution: c**
    a. Incorrect. Risk D would take precedence over risk A, as it has a higher probability of occurring despite the lower impact.
    b. Incorrect. This is the opposite of the correct order.
    c. Correct. This order ranks the risk by a combination of probability and impact.
    d. Incorrect. Risk D should be rated higher than risk C, due to probability and impact.

25. **Solution: c**
    a. Incorrect. This is not the best technique, as it takes only a two-pronged approach to risk management (that is, event and impact).
    b. Incorrect. This is not the best technique, as it does not take a comprehensive approach to risk management.
    c. Correct. This is the best response, as it takes a comprehensive approach to risk management; it not only considers the event and the impact, but also the causes.
    d. Incorrect. This option again takes a two-pronged approach and also talks about elimination of risks instead of mitigation of risks.

26. **Solution: a**
    a. Correct. Considering the strategic plan in the development of the internal audit plan will ensure that the audit objectives support the overall business objectives stated in the strategic plan.
    b. Incorrect. This action may make the internal audit plan fit better with the strategic plan but may not have an effect on management's approval.
    c. Incorrect. Although the chief audit executive (CAE) may make recommendations to improve the strategic plan, this is not the primary purpose of the CAE reviewing the plan.
    d. Incorrect. Although the importance of the internal audit function may be increased by such action, this is not the primary reason for the action.

27. **Solution: c**
    a. Incorrect. This would seldom have a long-range impact.
    b. Incorrect. This would rarely be a long-range concern.
    c. Correct. This would be a long-range planning topic because it affects market positioning.
    d. Incorrect. This is certainly a concern, but has less long-range impact than product quality.

28. **Solution: b**
    a. Incorrect. Determining how unacceptable risk should be managed is the role of management.
    b. Correct. Assurance services involve the internal auditor's objective assessment of management's risk management activities and the degree to which they are effective.
    c. Incorrect. Designing and updating the risk management process is the role of management.
    d. Incorrect. Designing controls would impair the internal auditor's independence.

29. **Solution: c**
    a. Incorrect. The total points are less than those of engagements 2 and 4.
    b. Incorrect. Total points are less than the other choices.
    c. Correct. Engagements 2 and 4 have the highest overall points.
    d. Incorrect. To perform engagements 3 and 4 would mean to bypass engagement 2, which ranks highest in overall points along with engagement 4.

30. **Solution: d**
    a. Incorrect. This choice involves the least total points.
    b. Incorrect. The total points are less than for engagements 3 and 4.
    c. Incorrect. The total points are less than for engagements 3 and 4.
    d. Correct. This has the highest total points, and the engagements have medium and high potentials for cost savings.

31. **Solution: a**
    a. Correct. Review and testing of the other department's procedures may reduce necessary audit coverage of the function or process.
    b. Incorrect. Concentrating on the function or process might lead to a duplication of efforts.
    c. Incorrect. The internal auditor can not rely on the work of others without verifying the results.
    d. Incorrect. The internal audit activity's overall responsibility for assessing the function or process is not affected by the other department's coverage.

32. Solution: b
    a. Incorrect. The responsibility for ensuring that the internal audit activity's professional and organizational responsibilities maximize the benefits that can be achieved from coordination with other assurance consulting activities lies with the chief audit executive, according to Practice Advisory 2050-1.3. Comments on this should always form part of any activity reports by the chief audit executive to the audit committee.
    b. Correct. Practice Advisory 2060-2.5 recommends that the chief audit executive provide the audit committee with information on the coordination with and oversight of other control and monitoring functions.
    c. Incorrect. The chief executive officer would not normally be responsible for planning, work, and coordination related to internal audit assurance and consulting engagements or coordination with other assurance and consulting activities.
    d. Incorrect. Not all other assurance and consulting activities are organizationally responsible to the audit committee for their work, and they may not have the opportunity to report information directly to the audit committee.

33. Solution: d
    a. Incorrect. Internal auditors should not attempt to influence regulators' interpretations of law.
    b. Incorrect. Internal auditors should not attempt to influence the scope of work of the regulatory examiners. This would be unethical and a violation of the *IIA Code of Ethics*.
    c. Incorrect. Internal auditors should not perform fieldwork for regulatory examiners.
    d. Correct. Internal auditors have immediate access to workpapers and reports, which can supply evidence of compliance testing to the regulatory examiners.

34. Solution: a
    a. Correct. This is an appropriate rationale.
    b. Incorrect. Such a listing might convince the chief audit executive of the need for risk assessment but is not provided by the process.
    c. Incorrect. This is used in the risk assessment process but is not the rationale for using risk assessment.
    d. Incorrect. This is one definition of risk.

35. Solution: b
    a. Incorrect. This is an important factor according to Practice Advisory 2010-1.4.
    b. Correct. While auditor skills should be considered in the planning process, audit needs – not auditor skill availability – should drive engagement work schedules in a risk-based audit plan.
    c. Incorrect. This is an important factor according to Practice Advisory 2010-1.4.
    d. Incorrect. This is an important factor according to Practice Advisory 2010-1.4.

36. Solution: c
    a. Incorrect. This factor would be considered in prioritizing the engagements.
    b. Incorrect. By reviewing staffing, prioritization of engagements, and expenses, operating benefits can be achieved.
    c. Correct. Practice Advisory 2010-1.2 states that the goals of the internal audit activity, as stated in specific operating plans and budgets, should include measurement criteria and targeted dates of accomplishment.
    d. Incorrect. Staffing for each engagement would include this consideration.

37. Solution: c
  a. Incorrect. This may lead to duplication in audit coverage.
  b. Incorrect. Internal auditing encompasses both financial and operational objectives and activities. Therefore, internal audit coverage could also be provided by external audit work which included primarily financial objectives and activities.
  c. Correct. Coordinating internal and external audit work helps to prevent duplication in coverage, thereby improving internal audit efficiency.
  d. Incorrect. External audit work is conducted in accordance with Generally Accepted Auditing Standards.

38. Solution: c
  a. Incorrect. Self-assessment questionnaires are a means of efficiently addressing the objectives of certain internal audits.
  b. Incorrect. Use of technology is an appropriate means of achieving efficiencies in audit execution.
  c. Correct. The audit schedule should only be reduced as a last resort once all other viable alternatives have been explored, including the request for additional resources.
  d. Incorrect. Using operating personnel with internal audit interest and corporate experience is an appropriate way to enhance internal audit resources.

39. Solution: a
  a. Correct. Senior management and the board of directors should be informed of the implications of gaps in audit coverage, including the review of compliance with applicable laws and regulations.
  b. Incorrect. The knowledge of incomplete audit coverage should not be known only to the internal audit activity.
  c. Incorrect. Compliance with material regulations may need to be reviewed on an annual basis.
  d. Incorrect. Audit coverage in other areas should not be automatically reduced. The internal audit activity may require additional resources to provide adequate coverage of risks.

40. Solution: c (III only)
  I. Incorrect. Requests from management and the audit committee should both be considered by the internal audit activity. Although an audit committee request is important, it is not always more important, nor does it always imply higher risk.
  II. Incorrect. Risk is measured by the potential exposure to the organization. The size of the departmental budget is an important determinant, but is not a sufficient determinant.
  III. Correct. Practice Advisory 2010-2 advises that the degree or materiality of exposure is an important component of risk.

41. Solution: b
  a. Incorrect. This does not conflict with the independence of the internal audit activity.
  b. Correct. In some circumstances, such as a product development team, the role of team leader or member may conflict with the independence attribute of the internal audit activity. The auditor can participate as a consultant to the team but should not participate as a team leader.
  c. Incorrect. To improve the ethical climate, the internal auditor should assume the role of ethics advocate, which therefore does not conflict with the independence of the internal audit activity.
  d. Incorrect. This does not conflict with the independence of the internal audit activity as the internal and external audit functions both share information and work collaboratively outside of the influence of management.

42. **Solution: d (I, II, III, and IV)**
    I. Correct. Evaluating whether ethics and values are promoted would contribute to corporate governance, according to Standard 2130.
    II. Correct. Evaluating the effectiveness of organizational performance management and accountability would contribute to corporate governance, according to Standard 2130.
    III. Correct. Evaluating how risk and control information is communicated would contribute to corporate governance, according to Standard 2130.
    IV. Correct. Evaluating the coordination of the external and internal auditors and management would contribute to corporate governance, according to Standard 2130.

43. **Solution: a**
    a. Correct. In a well-developed management system, the internal auditing function is used to provide a more direct benefit to line operations by providing feedback to operating management as well as to senior management.
    b. Incorrect. Emphasis should be placed on the audits of proposed products and systems. These early examinations could be used to determine the feasibility and/or desirability of changes before these changes are implemented.
    c. Incorrect. The role of the internal auditor involves interfacing with management at the operating level as well as at the senior level.
    d. Incorrect. Asset management would not be a primary focus of the internal audit activity.

44. **Solution: c**
    a. Incorrect. This is a purpose of audit planning.
    b. Incorrect. Correcting control weaknesses is a function of management, not of the internal auditor.
    c. Correct. This is the purpose stated in Practice Advisory 2100-1.1.
    d. Incorrect. This is a basic objective from a financial accounting and auditing perspective, but is not broad enough to cover the internal auditor's entire purpose for review.

45. **Solution: a**
    a. Correct. Operating management is responsible for risk management, executive management is responsible for oversight, and internal auditors serve in the capacity of oversight and advisory roles.
    b. Incorrect. Operating management performs the implementation role in risk management.
    c. Incorrect. Internal auditors are generally involved in the assurance and advisory role.
    d. Incorrect. Operating management is not involved in the oversight role.

46. **Solution: c**
    a. Incorrect. This is a responsibility of the chief audit executive (CAE), according to Standard 2020.
    b. Incorrect. This is a responsibility of the CAE, according to Standard 2050.
    c. Correct. Practice Advisory 2120.A1-1 states that this is the role of senior management, not the CAE.
    d. Incorrect. This is a responsibility of the CAE, according to Standard 2500.

47. **Solution: a**
    a. Correct. This is supported by Implementation Standard 2120.A4.
    b. Incorrect. In instances where management has not established the criteria, or if, in the auditor's opinion, the established criteria are judged less than adequate, the auditor should work with management to develop appropriate evaluation criteria.
    c. Incorrect. These are sources of information which will assist management in establishing goals and objective, relevant, meaningful criteria.
    d. Incorrect. Accounting or auditing standards would not be appropriate for this purpose.

48. **Solution: b**
    a. Incorrect. The internal audit activity performs this role. The board and management are responsible for the identification of an appropriate risk model and methodology.
    b. Correct. It is the role of management to ensure the timely implementation of the audit recommendations. The internal audit activity is responsible for the development of a timely procedure to monitor the disposition of the audit recommendations. The internal audit activity works with senior management and the audit committee to ensure that audit recommendations receive appropriate attention.
    c. Incorrect. The internal audit activity should monitor compliance with the corporate code of conduct set by the board and management.
    d. Incorrect. The internal audit activity is responsible for discussing significant financial, technical, and operational risks and exposures and the plans to minimize such risks.

49. **Solution: d**
    a. Incorrect. This assessment should be carried out at least annually.
    b. Incorrect. The board may request the chief audit executive (CAE) to participate in assessing the performance of the external auditors, and this may include assessment of independence.
    c. Incorrect. See answers "a" and "b".
    d. Correct. See answers "a" and "b".

50. **Solution: c**
    a. Incorrect. The chief executive officer (CEO) is a member of senior management. Other members of senior management may receive a final report that has been reviewed and approved by legal counsel.
    b. Incorrect. External auditors should not be contacted. External auditors may be given a final report that has been reviewed and approved by legal counsel.
    c. Correct. A draft of the proposed report on fraud or conflict-of-interest situations should be submitted to the chairman of the audit committee as a next step in light of the CEO's position in the company.
    d. Incorrect. Supporting documentation would be necessary before informing the audit committee or the board.

51. **Solution: a (II only)**
    I. Incorrect. The existence of a corporate code of ethics, by itself, does not ensure higher standards of ethical behavior. It must be complemented by follow-up policies and monitoring activities to ensure adherence to the code.
    II. Correct. A formalized corporate code of ethics presents objective criteria by which actions can be evaluated and would thus serve as criteria against which activities could be evaluated.
    III. Incorrect. Standards which would influence individual actions can occur in other places than the corporate code of ethics. For example, there may be defined policies regarding purchasing activities that may serve the same purpose as a code of ethics. These policies also serve as criteria against which activities may be evaluated.

52. **Solution: c**
    a. Incorrect. See answer "c".
    b. Incorrect. See answer "c".
    c. Correct. A chief audit executive should establish a follow-up process to monitor the adequacy, effectiveness, and timeliness of actions taken by management on reported engagement observations and recommendations, including those made by the external auditors and others.
    d. Incorrect. See answer "c".

53. Solution: a
   a. Correct. Organizations such as brokers, banks, and insurance companies may view risks as sufficiently critical to warrant continuous oversight and monitoring.
   b. Incorrect. A separate compliance function may have recommendations to help strengthen controls but this is not their primary purpose.
   c. Incorrect. Management is not independent as risk management is their direct responsibility.
   d. Incorrect. This will help respond to shareholder needs, but it is not the primary reason for establishing the compliance function.

54. Solution: d
   a. Incorrect. Senior management has an oversight role in risk management.
   b. Incorrect. The risk knowledge at the line level would be specific only to that area of the organization.
   c. Incorrect. The chief audit executive (CAE) does not have the responsibility for managing risk.
   d. Correct. The chief risk officer is most effective when supported by a specific team with the necessary expertise and experience related to organizational risk.

55. Solution: a
   a. Correct. The types and amounts of insurance should be supported by periodic appraisals.
   b. Incorrect. The determination of insurance coverage is not a function of the board of directors.
   c. Incorrect. The consumer price index generally does not provide an appropriate adjustment factor for fixed assets.
   d. Incorrect. Book values may not reflect the replacement or real value of an asset.

56. Solution: a (I only)
   I. Correct. Compensation systems influence behavior and should be considered an integral part of an organization's control structure. Thus, it should be considered as an important part of the control structure over derivatives trading.
   II. Incorrect. Compensation systems are part of the organization's control systems.
   III. Incorrect. Audits of the compensation systems can be combined with an audit over other functions that impact corporate bonuses.

57. Solution: d
   a. Incorrect. Corporate control mechanisms do include internal and external mechanisms.
   b. Incorrect. Management's compensation scheme is part of corporate control mechanisms.
   c. Incorrect. The dilution of shareholder's wealth resulting from employee stock options or employee stock bonuses is an accounting issue rather than a corporate governance issue.
   d. Correct. The board is ultimately responsible for the company's corporate governance, not the internal auditors.

58. Solution: b
   a. Incorrect. Insuring is a risk management activity.
   b. Correct. Hedging is the use of future contracts to limit risk exposure on exchange rates.
   c. Incorrect. Short-selling refers to the sales of commodities or shares of stocks.
   d. Incorrect. Factoring applies to discounting of accounts receivable.

59. Solution: c
   a. Incorrect. Risk management processes cannot totally guarantee achievement of objectives.
   b. Incorrect. Involvement of internal auditors in establishing control activities would impair their independence and objectivity.
   c. Correct. This option falls within the framework of risk management.
   d. Incorrect. Enterprise risk management is concerned not with selecting the best risk response, but with selecting the risk response that falls within the enterprise's risk appetite. It is also not selected by the audit committee but by the management team.

60. **Solution: c**
    a. Incorrect. The impact of risk is its consequence.
    b. Incorrect. Risk that is under control is managed risk.
    c. Correct. Residual risk is that risk left over after all controls and risk management techniques have been applied.
    d. Incorrect. The underlying risk is the absolute risk.

61. **Solution: d**
    a. Incorrect. Goods are seasonal and store space is limited. This is a constraint that is consistent with maximizing revenue and profitability for the organization.
    b. Incorrect. The product manager is evaluated based on sales and gross profit; thus, there is no conflict with performing both of these duties.
    c. Incorrect. Evaluating the product managers on gross profit and budgeted sales attaches responsibility to the manager.
    d. Correct. There is the possibility that goods could be diverted from the distribution center and not delivered to the appropriate retail store.

62. **Solution: a (I only)**
    I. Correct. The organization has two scarce resources to allocate: (a) its purchasing budget (constrained by financing ability) and (b) space available in retail stores. Thus, there is a need for a mechanism to allocate these two scarce resources to maximize the overall return to the organization. This is the proper mechanism.
    II. Incorrect. This is a preventive control, not a detective control.
    III. Incorrect. The gross profit evaluation is effective in evaluating the manager but does not address the two major constraints identified in statement I.

63. **Solution: c**
    a. Incorrect. Management is able to change the organization's members.
    b. Incorrect. Management is able to change the organization's structure.
    c. Correct. Environment is often determined by external forces, outside the direct control of the organization.
    d. Incorrect. Management is able to change the organization's technology.

64. **Solution: d**
    a. Incorrect. Eliminating checks does not represent an ongoing control
    b. Incorrect. Eliminating checks avoids instead of accepts the associated risk
    c. Incorrect. Risk is not transferred to anyone else; it is eliminated
    d. Correct. By eliminating checks, the organization avoids all risk associated with them.

65. **Solution: d**
    a. Incorrect. This is not a comprehensive approach to risk management.
    b. Incorrect. See answer "a".
    c. Incorrect. See answer "a".
    d. Correct. This is a comprehensive approach and will relate to risk management strategies across the enterprise.

66. **Solution: b**
    a. Incorrect. Real or imagined loss of jobs is a common reason for employees to resist any change.
    b. Correct. Employee training programs facilitate performing jobs in a new or different way.
    c. Incorrect. Members of work groups often exert peer pressure on one another to resist change, especially if social relationships are changed.
    d. Incorrect. Lack of communication and discussion of the need for change threatens the status quo.

67. Solution: c
   a, b, d. Incorrect. Each of these individual controls, and probably others as well, help management achieve its objective of preventing the release of waste water that does not meet permit limits or other conditions. These three controls each approach the risk in different ways. Analytical results are the criteria for the decision to discharge; keeping pollutants out of the waste water will help reduce concentrations and the degree of pretreatment needed; and equipment breakdown is less likely to occur if a preventive maintenance program is in place.
   c. Correct. Periodic dilution may not always prevent the release of pollutants which exceed the discharge limits.

68. Solution: a
   a. Correct. This is a cultural change because it involves a change in attitudes and mindset.
   b. Incorrect. Product change is change in a product's physical attributes and usefulness to customers.
   c. Incorrect. There is no change to systems and structures here.
   d. Incorrect. This is not an organizational change since it involves only quality assurance.

69. Solution: c
   a. Incorrect. Developing the plan then presenting it to the audit staff would not help reduce their resistance to change.
   b. Incorrect. Involving the CEO will not necessarily reduce the audit staff's resistance to change.
   c. Correct. Involving the staff in the change from the beginning will reduce their resistance to change.
   d. Incorrect. Involving the internal audit activity's clients will not necessarily reduce the audit staff's resistance to change.

70. Solution: c
   a. Incorrect. The manager has not dealt with the behavior and has missed the opportunity for coaching and conflict resolution with both staff members.
   b. Incorrect. Although one auditor has behaved improperly, both auditors allowed the situation to occur and both should be involved in its resolution to protect team morale and effectiveness.
   c. Correct. This allows both parties to discuss and resolve their differences under the supervision of the audit manager.
   d. Incorrect. This is not a matter for the entire team to address. The team may be advised after the resolution but should not be involved in a disciplinary action by the manager.

71. Solution: c
   a. Incorrect. Employees may be properly included on payroll, but the amounts paid may be unauthorized.
   b. Incorrect. Undelivered checks provide no evidence regarding the validity of the amounts.
   c. Correct. The employee's supervisor would be in the best position to ensure payment of the proper amount.
   d. Incorrect. Witnessing a payroll distribution would not assure that amounts paid are authorized.

72. Solution: a
   a. Correct. Supervisory review at the originating department level is one means of control over the number of items ordered.
   b. Incorrect. This procedure could lead to purchases of excess material because it does not consider future plans.
   c. Incorrect. This is a control for the risk of accepting unordered goods.
   d. Incorrect. This is a control for the risk of receiving an amount other than that ordered.

73. **Solution: d (II and IV only)**
    I.   Incorrect. This is a symptom of weak controls for achieving organizational goals and objectives, but not for safeguarding of assets.
    II. Correct. This is a symptom of weak controls for safeguarding of assets.
    III. Incorrect. This is a symptom of weak controls for achieving organizational goals and objectives, but not for safeguarding of assets.
    IV. Correct. Management's failure to take corrective action on past engagement observations, which related to safeguarding of assets, is a weakness related to safeguarding of assets.

74. **Solution: c**
    a. Incorrect. Total dollars committed would not detect favoritism shown to individual vendors.
    b. Incorrect. Detailed material specifications will not prevent buyer favoritism in placing orders.
    c. Correct. Periodic rotation of buyer assignments will limit the opportunity for any buyer to show favoritism to a particular supplier.
    d. Incorrect. The number of orders placed is not relevant to preventing favoritism.

75. **Solution: b**
    a. Incorrect. This would not ensure that raw materials are of sufficient quality.
    b. Correct. Specifications for materials purchased provide an objective means of determining that the materials meet the minimum quality level required for production.
    c. Incorrect. This would only help ensure that raw materials are used in the proper quantities.
    d. Incorrect. This would only permit proper determination of spoilage after raw materials have been used in production.

76. **Solution: a**
    a. Correct. Preventive controls are actions taken prior to the occurrence of transactions with the intent of stopping errors from occurring. Use of an approved vendor list is a control to prevent the use of unacceptable suppliers.
    b. Incorrect. A detective control is a control that identifies errors after they have occurred.
    c. Incorrect. Corrective controls correct the problems identified by detective controls.
    d. Incorrect. Monitoring controls are designed to ensure the quality of the control system's performance over time.

77. **Solution: a**
    a. Correct. Independent reconciliation of bank accounts is necessary for good internal control.
    b. Incorrect. This is not an important internal control consideration.
    c. Incorrect. Foreign currency translation rates are not computed, but instead verified. Having two employees in the same department perform the same task will not significantly enhance internal control.
    d. Incorrect. This is not an important internal control consideration.

78. **Solution: d**
    a. Incorrect. This may be used, but it is only one means in fulfilling the objective of a preliminary survey. Answer "d" is the most complete.
    b. Incorrect. See answer "a".
    c. Incorrect. See answer "a".
    d. Correct. Practice Advisory 2210.A1-1.2 states: "If appropriate, a survey should be conducted to become familiar with the activities, risks, and controls, to identify areas for engagement emphasis, and to invite comments and suggestions from engagement clients...."

79. **Solution: a**
    a. Correct. This preliminary survey information should prompt the auditor to identify the magnitude of such duplicate payments.
    b. Incorrect. Unrecorded liabilities would not result.
    c. Incorrect. The existence of duplicate payments is not related to a problem in the receiving area.
    d. Incorrect. Duplicate payments are not overpayments; they are exceptions and should be handled as such.

80. **Solution: d**
    a. Incorrect. See answer "d".
    b. Incorrect. See answer "d".
    c. Incorrect. See answer "d".
    d. Correct. All of the procedures should be performed. See Practice Advisory 2210.A1-1, which describes a preliminary review.

81. **Solution: b**
    a. Incorrect. These trends would not result in scope expansion, because they are compatible.
    b. Correct. These trends may indicate inflated sales figures.
    c. Incorrect. These trends would not result in scope expansion, because they are compatible.
    d. Incorrect. These trends would not result in scope expansion, because they are compatible.

82. **Solution: c**
    a. Incorrect. It is important to maintain a broad scope and not reduce scope prematurely.
    b. Incorrect. While the auditor may be able to contribute to the environmental, health, and safety (EHS) manager's knowledge of pertinent air-quality matters, it is much more important during this phase of the engagement to learn what the manager does.
    c. Correct. The auditor should ensure that the fieldwork is designed to identify potential instances of noncompliance and, in the closing conference, should recommend additional training for the EHS manager.
    d. Incorrect. It is not appropriate for an auditor to report violations or potential violations to regulatory agencies. Such matters are the responsibility of company counsel.

83. **Solution: b**
    a. Incorrect. This specifies part of an engagement program step.
    b. Correct. This is something the audit engagement is to accomplish. It is also specific since it ties the inventory balance to the criterion of meeting projected customer needs.
    c. Incorrect. This is an engagement program step.
    d. Incorrect. This is a specification for the engagement final communication.

84. **Solution: c**
    a. Incorrect. Since new financial instruments are very risky, the first step of such an engagement should be to determine the nature of policies established for the investments.
    b. Incorrect. Oversight by a management committee is an important control. Therefore, the auditor should determine the nature of the oversight set up to monitor and authorize such investments.
    c. Correct. Although this might be informational, there is no need to develop a comparison of investment returns with other organizations. Indeed, some financial investment scandals show that such comparisons can be highly misleading because high returns were due to taking on a high level of risk. Also, this is not a test of the adequacy of the controls.
    d. Incorrect. A fundamental control concept over cash-like assets is that someone establishes a mechanism to monitor the risks.

85. **Solution: a**
    a. Correct. This is what is required by the *Standards* (Implementation Standard 2120.A4 and related Practice Advisory 2120.A4-1).
    b. Incorrect. The auditor should seek to understand the operating standards as they are applied to the organization. Also, best practices may produce overly high standards.
    c. Incorrect. The *Standards* state that if internal auditors must interpret standards, they should seek agreement with the engagement client.
    d. Incorrect. The auditor should first seek to gain an understanding with the departmental manager on the appropriate standards.

86. **Solution: a**
    a. Correct. If the preliminary evaluation indicates control problems, the auditor usually decides to perform some expanded testing.
    b. Incorrect. If a flowchart were necessary, the auditor would have prepared one during the preliminary evaluation.
    c. Incorrect. The auditor is not ready to make a report until more work has been performed.
    d. Incorrect. Auditors do not implement controls; that is a function of management.

87. **Solution: b**
    a. Incorrect. Predefined spending levels would probably already include the fraudulent amounts and would only limit the size of the fraud.
    b. Correct. Additional authorization would be the most likely choice in preventing the fraud.
    c. Incorrect. The bill of lading would agree with the purchase order. The quantity received (verified by a third party) should be compared to both the bill of lading and the purchase order.
    d. Incorrect. The computer matching would only verify the fraudulent paperwork.

88. **Solution: c**
    a. Incorrect. The current quarter's expense would equal the prior period's activity unless the manager just started this fraud. The auditor has no information on how long this might have been occurring.
    b. Incorrect. Physical testing would not locate nonexistent parts that have already been charged to maintenance.
    c. Correct. An analysis of repair parts charged to maintenance would quantify the excessive number of items and detect that abuse may be occurring.
    d. Incorrect. Lack of segregation of duties allowed the fraud to occur. The manager was authorized to process both the purchase and receipt, so the test would only verify the fraudulent paperwork.

89. **Solution: b**
    a. Incorrect. The engagement may be conducted under a scope limitation.
    b. Correct. Practice Advisory 1130-1.3 states that a scope limitation and its potential effects should be communicated to the audit committee of the board of directors.
    c. Incorrect. A scope limitation would not necessarily cause the need for more frequent audit engagements.
    d. Incorrect. A scope limitation would not necessarily cause the need for more experienced personnel.

90. **Solution: a**
    a. Correct. After ten years, the program's effectiveness needs to be assessed. If the auditor assesses the effects of the incompleteness of the data as the auditor evaluates it and disclaims the reliability, the auditor will provide readers with some assessment of effectiveness without misleading readers about the interpretability of the data.
    b. Incorrect. The organization has already asserted that the data are incomplete. This step would be redundant.
    c. Incorrect. Many times auditors need to work with imperfect data. A program that has continued for ten years needs assessment. As long as the auditor assesses the effects of the incomplete data and disclaims the reliability of the data clearly in the report, the analysis may prove useful without being misleading.
    d. Incorrect. See answer "c".

91. **Solution: a**
    a. Correct. Most fraud perpetrators would attempt to conceal their theft by charging it against an expense account.
    b. Incorrect. Debiting the stolen asset account would be going in the wrong direction to conceal an asset theft.
    c. Incorrect. An entry decreasing revenue would be unusual and would stand out.
    d. Incorrect. This entry would not permanently conceal the fraud. It would simply shift the unreconcilible balance to another asset account.

92. **Solution: b**
    a. Incorrect. A group has a better chance of successfully perpetrating an irregularity than does an individual employee.
    b. Correct. A good system of internal controls is likely to expose an irregularity if it is perpetrated by one employee, without the aid of others.
    c. Incorrect. Management can often override controls, singularly or in groups.
    d. Incorrect. Management can often override controls, singularly or in groups.

93. **Solution: b**
    a. Incorrect. This procedure would be useful only to determine if the cause was due to overstated inventory.
    b. Correct. An analysis of operations would be relevant in determining the efficiency of operations.
    c. Incorrect. Changes in equipment may signal an improvement in efficiency, but this approach would not be as relevant as that in answer "b".
    d. Incorrect. This procedure would be relevant in determining the correctness of raw materials purchases, but would not provide any evidence regarding the efficiency of operations.

94. **Solution: b**
    a. Incorrect. Access controls are tangential to the issue. Authorized, but incorrect data, could also be the problem.
    b. Correct. This procedure would establish the cause of the problem.
    c. Incorrect. This would provide useful information, but it is not as comprehensive as answer "b". Further, answer "b" provides more information on the cause.
    d. Incorrect. This tests only one source of the data inaccuracy (that is, the input of production data); other sources of potential error are ignored.

95. Solution: a
a. Correct. This is the most appropriate procedure because: (a) the auditor has already determined that there is a concern; and (b) this procedure results in a direct comparison of current parts requirements with purchase orders being generated. Differences can be identified and corrective action taken.
b. Incorrect. This procedure provides evidence that all items entered are processed. Comparison with currently generated purchase orders does not provide evidence on whether the correct parts are being ordered.
c. Incorrect. Generalized audit software is a good method to identify an inventory problem. However, the excess inventory may not be the result of a revised production technique. Answer "a" more directly addresses the audit concern.
d. Incorrect. This procedure provides evidence on the input of data into the system, but does not provide evidence on whether changes in the production process have been implemented.

96. Solution: a
a. Correct. The results of a financial audit engagement would be the least relevant factor in prioritizing the auditors' tasks.
b. Incorrect. Fraud is one of the major factors to be considered in analyzing risk and identifying audit activities.
c. Incorrect. The increase in expenditures provides a benchmark for potential exposure or loss to the organization.
d. Incorrect. Fines imposed by regulatory agencies could represent a significant risk.

97. Solution: a
a. Correct. Time budgets should be appraised for revision after the preliminary survey and preparation of the engagement program.
b. Incorrect. When a deficiency has been substantiated, no further audit work is required.
c. Incorrect. The assignment of inexperienced staff should have no effect on the time budget.
d. Incorrect. Expanded tests should have no effect on the time budget; the budget would have already been expanded as necessary.

98. Solution: d
a. Incorrect. The internal auditor may be responsible if assigned to this engagement, but does not have ultimate responsibility.
b. Incorrect. The audit committee is responsible for ensuring that the objectives of the annual audit plan are met, but is not responsible for each audit engagement's objectives.
c. Incorrect. The internal audit supervisor may be responsible if assigned to this engagement, but does not have ultimate responsibility
d. Correct. Per Practice Advisory 2340-1, the chief audit executive is responsible for supervision, including determining that engagement objectives are being met.

99. Solution: b
a. Incorrect. A standardized engagement program would be appropriate for use in a minimally changing operating environment.
b. Correct. A standardized engagement program would not be appropriate for a complex or changing operating environment because the engagement objectives and related work steps may no longer have relevance.
c. Incorrect. A standardized engagement program could be used to audit multiple branches with similar operations.
d. Incorrect. A standardized engagement program would be acceptable for conducting subsequent inventory audit engagements at the same location.

100. Solution: a
   a. Correct. A tailored program will be more relevant to an operation than will a generalized program.
   b. Incorrect. A generalized program cannot take into account variations resulting from changing circumstances and varied conditions.
   c. Incorrect. A generalized program cannot take into account variations in circumstances and conditions.
   d. Incorrect. Every aspect of an operation need not be examined — only those likely to conceal problems and difficulties.

END OF PART I SOLUTIONS

Certified Internal Auditor (CIA) Model Exam Questions

Part II - Conducting the Internal Audit Engagement

Part II Model Exam Questions: 100

Questions on actual CIA Exam Part II: 125
(see explanation in "Foreword" on page iii)

Time allowed for completion of CIA Exam Part II: 210 minutes

Instructions such as those that follow will be listed on the cover of each CIA examination. Please read them carefully.

1. Place your candidate number on the answer sheet in the space provided.
2. Do not place extraneous marks on the answer sheet.
3. Be certain that changes to answers are **completely** erased.
4. All references to the *Professional Practices Framework* refer to The IIA's *Professional Practices Framework*, which includes the *Standards* and the *Practice Advisories*.

All references to *Standards* refer to the *International Standards for the Professional Practice of Internal Auditing* outlined in The IIA's *Professional Practices Framework*.

5. The following statistical sampling terms are used synonymously: a. Dollar-unit, monetary-unit, probability proportional to size; b. Confidence level and reliability; and c. Precision and allowance for sampling risk.

Failure to follow these instructions and the "Instructions to Candidates" guidelines could adversely affect both your right to receive the results of this examination and your future participation in the Certified Internal Auditor program.

All papers submitted in completion of any part of this examination become the sole property of The Institute of Internal Auditors, Inc. Candidates may not disclose the contents of this exam unless expressly authorized by the Certification Department.

1. A specific objective of an audit of a company's expenditure cycle is to determine if all goods paid for have been received and charged to the correct account. This objective would address which of the following primary objectives identified in the *Standards*?

   I. Reliability and integrity of financial and operational information.
   II. Compliance with laws, regulations, and contracts.
   III. Effectiveness and efficiency of operations.
   IV. Safeguarding of assets.

   a. I and II only.
   b. I and IV only.
   c. I, II, and IV only.
   d. II, III, and IV only.

2. Which of the following would be permissible under the *IIA Code of Ethics*?
   a. In response to a subpoena, an auditor appeared in a court of law and disclosed confidential, audit-related information that could potentially damage the auditor's organization.
   b. An auditor used audit-related information in a decision to buy stock issued by the employer corporation.
   c. After praising an employee in a recent audit engagement communication, an auditor accepted a gift from the employee.
   d. An auditor did not report significant observations about illegal activity to the board because management indicated that it would resolve the issue.

3. An internal auditor who encounters an ethical dilemma not explicitly addressed by the *IIA Code of Ethics* should always:
   a. Seek counsel from an independent attorney to determine the personal consequences of potential actions.
   b. Take action consistent with the principles embodied in the *IIA Code of Ethics*.
   c. Seek the counsel of the audit committee before deciding on an action.
   d. Act consistently with the employing organization's code of ethics even if such action would not be consistent with the *IIA Code of Ethics*.

4. An auditor uncovers a plan to overstate inventory and thereby increase reported profits for a division. The auditor has substantial evidence that the divisional manager was aware of and approved the plan to overstate inventory. There is also some evidence that the manager may have been responsible for the implementation of the plan. The auditor should:
   a. Continue to conduct interviews with subordinates until a definite case is made, and then report the case to the audit committee.
   b. Inform senior management and the audit committee of the findings and discuss possible further investigation.
   c. Inform the divisional manager of the auditor's suspicions and obtain the manager's explanation of the findings before pursuing the matter further.
   d. Document the case thoroughly and report the suspicions to the external auditor for further review.

5. Data-gathering activities such as interviewing operating personnel, identifying standards to be used to evaluate performance, and assessing risks inherent in a department's operations are typically performed in which phase of an audit engagement?
   a. Fieldwork.
   b. Preliminary survey.
   c. Engagement program development.
   d. Examination and evaluation of evidence.

6. Which of the following best describes an auditor's responsibility after noting some indicators of fraud?
   a. Expand activities to determine whether an investigation is warranted.
   b. Report the possibility of fraud to senior management and ask how to proceed.
   c. Consult with external legal counsel to determine the course of action to be taken.
   d. Report the matter to the audit committee and request funding for outside specialists to help investigate the possible fraud.

7. Which of the following would be **least** useful in predicting the amount of uncollectible accounts for an organization?
   a. Published economic indices indicating a general business downturn.
   b. Dollar amounts of accounts actually written off by the organization for each of the past six months.
   c. Total monthly sales for each of the past six months.
   d. Written forecasts from the credit manager regarding expected future cash collections.

8. To be sufficient, audit evidence should be:
   a. Well-documented and cross-referenced in the workpapers.
   b. Based on references that are considered reliable.
   c. Directly related to the engagement observation and include all of the elements of an engagement observation.
   d. Convincing enough for a prudent person to reach the same conclusion as the auditor.

9. Which of the following examples of audit evidence is the most persuasive?
   a. Real estate deeds, which were properly recorded with a government agency.
   b. Canceled checks written by the treasurer and returned from a bank.
   c. Time cards for employees, which are stored by a manager.
   d. Vendor invoices filed by the accounting department.

10. Competent evidence is best defined as evidence which:
    a. Is reasonably free from error and bias and faithfully represents that which it purports to represent.
    b. Is obtained by observing people, property, and events.
    c. Is supplementary to other evidence already gathered and which tends to strengthen or confirm it.
    d. Proves an intermediate fact, or group of facts, from which still other facts can be inferred.

11. Which of the following represents the most competent evidence that trade receivables actually exist?
    a. Positive confirmations.
    b. Sales invoices.
    c. Receiving reports.
    d. Bills of lading.

12. The following represents accounts receivable information for a corporation for a three-year period:

	Year One	Year Two	Year Three
Net accounts receivable as a percentage of total assets	23.4%	27.3%	30.8%
Accounts receivable turnover ratio	6.98	6.05	5.21

    All of the following are plausible explanations for these changes **except**:
    a. Fictitious sales may have been recorded.
    b. Credit and collection procedures have become ineffective.
    c. Allowance for bad debts is understated.
    d. Sales returns for credit have been overstated.

13. A company's accounts receivable turnover rate decreased from 7.3 to 4.3 over the last three years. What is the most likely cause for the decrease?
    a. An increase in the discount offered for early payment.
    b. A more liberal credit policy.
    c. A change in net payment due from 30 to 25 days.
    d. Increased cash sales.

14. Reviewing an edit listing of payroll changes processed during each payroll cycle would most likely reveal:
    a. Undetected errors in the payroll rates of new employees.
    b. Inaccurate payroll deductions.
    c. Labor hours charged to the wrong account in the cost reporting system.
    d. A failure to offer employees an opportunity to contribute to their pension plan.

15. What does the following scattergram suggest?

    a. Sales revenue is inversely related to training costs.
    b. The training program is not effective.
    c. Training costs do not affect sales revenue.
    d. Several data points are incorrectly plotted.

16. Which of the following statements are correct regarding audit engagement workpaper documentation for a fraud investigation?

    I. All incriminating evidence should be included in the workpapers.
    II. All important testimonial evidence should be reviewed to ensure that it provides sufficient basis for the conclusions reached.
    III. If interviews are held with a suspected perpetrator, written transcripts or statements should be included in the workpapers.

    a. I only.
    b. II only.
    c. II and III only.
    d. I, II, and III.

17. Workpaper summaries, if prepared, can be used to:
    a. Promote efficient workpaper review by internal audit supervisors.
    b. Replace the detailed workpaper files for permanent retention.
    c. Serve as an engagement final communication to senior management.
    d. Document the full development of engagement observations and recommendations.

18. Which of the following represents appropriate evidence of supervisory review of engagement workpapers?

    I. A supervisor's initials on each workpaper.
    II. An engagement workpaper review checklist.
    III. A memorandum specifying the nature, extent, and results of the supervisory review of workpapers.
    IV. Performance appraisals that assess the quality of workpapers prepared by auditors.

    a. II and IV only.
    b. I, II, and III only.
    c. I, III, and IV only.
    d. I, II, III, and IV.

19. Which of the following most completely describes the appropriate content of engagement workpapers?
    a. Objectives, procedures, and conclusions.
    b. Purpose, criteria, techniques, and conclusions.
    c. Objectives, procedures, facts, conclusions, and recommendations.
    d. Subject, purpose, sampling information, and analysis.

20. Which of the following situations is most likely to be the subject of a written interim report to the engagement client?
    a. Seventy percent of the planned audit work has been completed with no significant adverse observations.
    b. The auditors have decided to substitute survey procedures for some of the planned detailed review of certain records.
    c. The engagement program has been expanded because of indications of possible fraud.
    d. Open burning at a subsidiary plant poses a prospective violation of pollution regulations.

Use the following information to answer questions 21 through 23.

A medium-sized municipality provides 8.5 billion gallons of water per year for 31,000 customers. The water meters are replaced at least every five years to ensure accurate billing. The water department tracks unmetered water to identify water consumption that is not being billed. The department recently issued the following water activity report:

Activity	Month One	Month Two	Month Three	Actual 1st Quarter	1st Quarter Goal
Meters Replaced	475	400	360	1,235	1,425
Leaks Reported	100	100	85	285	
Leaks Repaired	100	100	85	285	100%
Unmetered Water	2%	6%	2%	4%	2%

21. Based on the activity reported for the meter replacement program, an internal auditor would conclude that:
   a. Established operating standards are understood and are being met.
   b. Any corrective action needed has probably been taken during the quarter.
   c. Deviations from the goal should be analyzed and corrected.
   d. Meters should be changed every three years.

22. Based on the activity reported for leaks repaired in the first quarter, an internal auditor would conclude that:
   a. Established operating standards are understood and are being met.
   b. Deviations from the goal should be analyzed and corrective action should be taken.
   c. The operating standard should be changed.
   d. The leak-repair program is overstaffed.

23. Based on the activity reported for the unmetered water, an internal auditor would conclude that:
   a. Established operating standards are understood and are being met.
   b. Further audit investigation of unmetered water is not warranted.
   c. Deviations from the goal were probably not corrected.
   d. The operating standard should be changed.

24. While testing a division's compliance with company affirmative-action policies, an auditor found that:
   (1) Five percent of the employees are from minority groups.
   (2) No one from a minority group has been hired in the past year.
   The most appropriate conclusion for the auditor to reach is that:
   a. Insufficient evidence exists of compliance with affirmative-action policies.
   b. The division is violating the company's policies.
   c. The company's policies cannot be audited and hence cannot be enforced.
   d. With five percent of its employees from minority groups, the division is effectively complying.

25. Recommendations should be included in audit reports in order to:
   a. Provide management with options for addressing audit findings.
   b. Ensure that problems are resolved in the manner suggested by the auditor.
   c. Minimize the amount of time required to correct audit findings.
   d. Guarantee that audit findings are addressed, regardless of cost.

26. According to the *Professional Practices Framework*, which of the following is part of the minimum requirements for an engagement final communication?
   I.   Background information.
   II. Purpose of the engagement.
   III. Engagement scope.
   IV. Results of the engagement.
   V.   Summaries.

   a. I, II, and III only.
   b. I, III, and V only.
   c. II, III, and IV only.
   d. II, IV, and V only.

27. Which of the following would **not** be considered a primary objective of a closing or exit conference?
   a. To resolve conflicts.
   b. To discuss the engagement observations and recommendations.
   c. To identify concerns for future audit engagements.
   d. To identify management's actions and responses to the engagement observations and recommendations.

28. During a review of purchasing operations, an auditor found that procedures in use did not agree with stated company procedures. However, audit tests revealed that the procedures in use represented an increase in efficiency and a decrease in processing time, without a discernible decrease in control. The auditor should:
   a. Report the lack of adherence to documented procedures as an operational deficiency.
   b. Develop a flowchart of the new procedures and include it in the report to management.
   c. Report the change and suggest that the change in procedures be documented.
   d. Suspend the completion of the engagement until the engagement client documents the new procedures.

29. The primary reason for having written formal audit reports is to:
   a. Provide an opportunity for engagement client response.
   b. Document the corrective actions required of senior management.
   c. Provide a formal means by which the external auditor assesses potential reliance on the internal audit activity.
   d. Record observations and recommended courses of action.

30. Which of the following is the best approach for obtaining feedback from engagement clients on the quality of internal audit work?
   a. Ask questions during the exit interviews and send copies of the documented responses to the clients.
   b. Call engagement clients after the exit interviews and send copies of the documented responses to the clients.
   c. Distribute questionnaires to selected engagement clients shortly before preparing the internal audit annual activity report.
   d. Provide questionnaires to engagement clients at the beginning of each engagement and request that the clients complete and return them after the engagements.

31. When conducting a performance appraisal of an internal auditor who has been a below-average performer, it is **not** appropriate to:
   a. Notify the internal auditor of the upcoming appraisal several days in advance.
   b. Use objective, impartial language.
   c. Use generalizations.
   d. Document the appraisal.

32. An auditor is scheduled to audit payroll controls for a company that has recently outsourced its processing to an information service bureau. What action should the auditor take, considering the outsourcing decision?
   a. Review the controls over payroll in both the company and the service bureau.
   b. Review only the company's controls over data sent to and received from the service bureau.
   c. Review only the controls over payments to the service bureau based on the contract.
   d. Cancel the engagement, because the processing is being performed outside of the organization.

33. Upon obtaining factual documentation of unethical business conduct by the vice president to whom the chief audit executive (CAE) reports, the CAE should:
   a. Conduct an investigation to determine the extent of the vice president's involvement in the unethical acts.
   b. Confront the vice president with the facts before proceeding.
   c. Schedule an audit of the business function involved.
   d. Report the facts to the chief executive officer and the audit committee.

34. Which of the following control procedures would be the **least** effective in preventing frauds in which purchase orders are issued to fictitious vendors?
   a. Require that all purchases be made from an authorized vendor list maintained independently of the individual placing the purchase order.
   b. Require that only preapproved vendors be paid for purchases, based on actual production.
   c. Require contracts with all major vendors from whom production components are purchased.
   d. Require that total purchases from all vendors for a month not exceed the total budgeted purchases for that month.

35. When interviewing an individual suspected of a fraud, the interviewer should:
    a. Ensure the suspect's supervisor is present during the interview.
    b. Lock the door to ensure no one will interrupt the interview.
    c. Pay attention to the wording choices of the suspect.
    d. Ask if the suspect committed the fraud.

36. Which phrase best describes a control-based control self-assessment process?
    a. Evaluating, updating, and streamlining selected control processes.
    b. Examining how well controls are working in managing key risks.
    c. Analyzing the gap between control design and control frameworks.
    d. Determining the cost-effectiveness of controls.

37. Determination of cost savings is most likely to be an objective of:
    a. Program audit engagements.
    b. Financial audit engagements.
    c. Compliance audit engagements.
    d. Operational audit engagements.

38. An auditor is considering developing a questionnaire to research employee attitudes toward control procedures. Which of the following represents the **least** important criteria in designing the questionnaire?
    a. Questions should be worded to ensure a valid interpretation by the respondents.
    b. Questions should be reliably worded so that they measure what was intended to be measured.
    c. The length of the questionnaire should be minimized in order to increase the response rate.
    d. Questions should be worded such that a "No" answer indicates a problem.

39. A performance audit engagement typically involves:
    a. Review of financial statement information, including the appropriateness of various accounting treatments.
    b. Tests of compliance with policies, procedures, laws, and regulations.
    c. Appraisal of the environment and comparison against established criteria.
    d. Evaluation of organizational and departmental structures, including assessments of process flows.

40. An engagement objective is to determine if a company's accounts payable contain all outstanding liabilities. Which of the following audit procedures would **not** be relevant for this objective?
    a. Examine supporting documentation of subsequent (after-period) cash disbursements and verify period of liability.
    b. Send confirmations, including zero-balance accounts, to vendors with whom the company normally does business.
    c. Select a sample of accounts payable from the accounts payable listing and verify the supporting receiving reports, purchase orders, and invoices.
    d. Trace receiving reports issued before the period end to the related vendor invoices and accounts payable listing.

41. An internal audit team is performing a due diligence audit to assess plans for a potential merger/acquisition. Which of the following would be the **least** valid reason for a company to merge with or acquire another company?
    a. To diversify risk.
    b. To respond to government policy.
    c. To reduce labor costs.
    d. To increase stock prices.

42. Which of the following procedures would be appropriate for testing whether cost overruns on a construction project were caused by the contractor improperly accounting for costs related to contract change orders?

    I. Verify that the contractor has not charged change orders with costs that have already been billed to the original contract.
    II. Determine if the contractor has billed for original contract work that was canceled as a result of change orders.
    III. Verify that the change orders were properly approved by management.

    a. I only.
    b. III only.
    c. I and II only.
    d. I and III only.

43. Which of the following would be the most appropriate starting point for a compliance evaluation of software licensing requirements for an organization with more than 15,000 computer workstations?
    a. Determine if software installation is controlled centrally or distributed throughout the organization.
    b. Determine what software packages have been installed on the organization's computers and the number of each package installed.
    c. Determine how many copies of each software package have been purchased by the organization.
    d. Determine what mechanisms have been installed for monitoring software usage.

44. A transportation department maintains its vehicle inventory and maintenance records in a database. Which of the following audit procedures is most appropriate for evaluating the accuracy of the database information?
    a. Verify a sample of the records extracted from the database with supporting documentation.
    b. Submit batches of test transactions through the current system and verify with expected results.
    c. Simulate normal processing by using test programs.
    d. Use program tracing to show how, and in what sequence, program instructions are processed in the system.

45. Systems development audit engagements include reviews at various points to ensure that development is properly controlled and managed. The reviews should include all of the following **except**:
    a. Conducting a technical feasibility study on the available hardware, software, and technical resources.
    b. Examining the level of user involvement at each stage of implementation.
    c. Verifying the use of controls and quality assurance techniques for program development, conversion, and testing.
    d. Determining if system, user, and operations documentation conforms to formal standards.

46. Which of the following should be reviewed before designing any system elements in a top-down approach to new systems development?
    a. Types of processing systems used by competitors.
    b. Computer equipment needed by the system.
    c. Information needs of managers for planning and control.
    d. Controls in place over the current system.

47. In conducting an audit of an organization's disaster recovery capability, which of the following would an auditor consider to be the most serious weakness?
    a. Tests utilize recovery scripts.
    b. Hot-site contracts are two years old.
    c. Backup media are stored on-site.
    d. Only a few systems are tested annually.

48. If electronic funds transfer (EFT) is used to pay vendor invoices, which of the following computer-assisted audit procedures would an auditor use to determine if any payments were made twice?

    I. Identification of EFT transactions to the same vendor for the same dollar amount.
    II. Extraction of EFT transactions with unauthorized vendor codes.
    III. Testing of EFT transactions for reasonableness.
    IV. Searching for EFT transactions with duplicate purchase order numbers.

    a. I and II only.
    b. I and IV only.
    c. II and III only.
    d. III and IV only.

49. During an operational audit engagement, an auditor compared the inventory turnover rate of a subsidiary with established industry standards in order to:
    a. Evaluate the accuracy of internal financial reports.
    b. Test controls designed to safeguard assets.
    c. Determine compliance with corporate procedures regarding inventory levels.
    d. Assess performance and indicate where additional audit work may be needed.

50. An organization uses electronic data interchange and on-line systems rather than paper-based documents for purchase orders, receiving reports, and invoices. Which of the following audit procedures would an auditor use to determine if invoices are paid only for goods received and at approved prices?
    a. Select a statistical sample of major vendors and trace the amounts paid to specific invoices.
    b. Use generalized audit software to select a sample of payments and match purchase orders, invoices, and receiving reports stored on the computer using a common reference.
    c. Select a monetary-unit sample of accounts payable and confirm the amounts directly with the vendors.
    d. Use generalized audit software to identify all receipts for a particular day and trace the receiving reports to checks issued.

51. Which of the following is true of benchmarking?
    a. It is typically accomplished by comparing an organization's performance with the performance of its closest competitors.
    b. It can be performed using either qualitative or quantitative comparisons.
    c. It is normally limited to manufacturing operations and production processes.
    d. It is accomplished by comparing an organization's performance to that of the best-performing organizations.

52. If a financial institution overstated revenue by charging too much of each loan payment to interest income and too little to repayment of principal, which of the following audit procedures would be **least** likely to detect the error?
    a. Performing an analytical review by comparing interest income this period as a percentage of the loan portfolio with the interest income percentage for the prior period.
    b. Using an integrated test facility (ITF) and submitting interest payments for various loans in the ITF portfolio to determine if they are recorded correctly.
    c. Using test data and submitting interest payments for various loans in the test portfolio to determine if they are recorded correctly.
    d. Using generalized audit software to select a random sample of loan payments made during the period, calculating the correct posting amounts, and tracing the postings that were made to the various accounts.

53. A hospital is evaluating the purchase of software to integrate a new cost accounting system with its existing financial accounting system. Which of the following describes the most effective way for the internal audit activity to be involved in the procurement process?
    a. The internal audit activity evaluates whether performance specifications are consistent with the hospital's needs.
    b. The internal audit activity evaluates whether the application design meets internal development and documentation standards.
    c. The internal audit activity determines whether the prototyped model is validated and reviewed with users before production use begins.
    d. The internal audit activity has no involvement since the system has already been developed externally.

54. Senior management of an entity has requested that the internal audit activity provide ongoing internal control training for all managerial personnel. This is best addressed by:
    a. A formal consulting engagement agreement.
    b. An informal consulting engagement agreement.
    c. A special consulting engagement agreement.
    d. An emergency consulting engagement agreement.

55. A consulting activity appropriately performed by the internal audit function is:
    a. Designing systems of control.
    b. Drafting procedures for systems of control.
    c. Reviewing systems of control before implementation.
    d. Installing systems of control.

56. As part of a preliminary survey of the purchasing function, an auditor read the department's policies and procedures manual. The auditor concluded that the manual described the processing steps well and contained an appropriate internal control design. The next engagement objective was to determine the operating effectiveness of internal controls. Which procedure would be most appropriate in meeting this objective?
    a. Prepare a flowchart.
    b. Prepare a system narrative.
    c. Perform a test of controls.
    d. Perform a substantive test.

57. An auditor reviewing an organization's plan for developing a performance scorecard. Which of the following potential performance measures should the auditor recommend **excluding** from the performance scorecard?
    a. Product innovation.
    b. Market share.
    c. Customer satisfaction.
    d. Employee development.

58. A sales department has been giving away expensive items in conjunction with new product sales to stimulate demand. The promotion seems successful, but management believes the cost may be too high and has asked for a review by the internal audit activity. Which of the following procedures would be the **least** useful to determine the effectiveness of the promotion?
    a. Comparing product sales during the promotion period with sales during a similar non-promotion period.
    b. Comparing the unit cost of the products sold before and during the promotion period.
    c. Performing an analysis of marginal revenue and marginal cost for the promotion period, compared to the period before the promotion.
    d. Performing a review of the sales department's benchmarks used to determine the success of a promotion.

59. Sales representatives for a manufacturing company are reimbursed for 100 percent of their cellular telephone bills. Cellular telephone costs vary significantly from representative to representative and from month to month, complicating the budgeting and forecasting processes. Management has requested that the internal auditors develop a method for controlling these costs. Which of the following would most appropriately be included in the scope of the consulting project?
    a. Control self-assessment involving sales representatives.
    b. Benchmarking with other cellular telephone users.
    c. Business process review of procurement and payables routines.
    d. Performance measurement and design of the budgeting and forecasting processes.

60. An organization wants to improve on its performance measures for a new business line. Which type of benchmarking is most likely to provide information useful for this purpose?
    a. Functional.
    b. Competitive.
    c. Generic.
    d. Internal.

61. One of the audit objectives for a manufacturing company is to verify that all rework is reviewed by the production engineer. Which of the following audit procedures would provide the best evidence for meeting this objective?
    a. Trace a sample of entries in the rework log to remedial action taken.
    b. Trace a sample of rework orders to entries in the rework log.
    c. Trace a sample of entries in the review log to rework orders.
    d. Trace a sample of rework orders to entries in the review log.

62. An audit of accounts payable found that the individuals responsible for maintaining the vendor master file could also enter vendor invoices into the accounts payable system. During the exit conference, management agreed to correct this problem. When performing a follow-up engagement of accounts payable, the auditor should expect to find that management had:
    a. Transferred the individuals who maintained the vendor master file to another department to ensure responsibilities were appropriately segregated.
    b. Compared the vendor and employee master files to determine if any unauthorized vendors had been added to the vendor master file.
    c. Modified the access control system to prevent employees from both entering invoices and approving payments.
    d. Modified the accounts payable system to prevent individuals who maintained the vendor master file from entering invoices.

63. An audit found that the cost of some material installed on capital projects had been transferred to the inventory account because the capital budget had been exceeded. Which of the following would be an appropriate technique for the internal audit activity to use to monitor this situation?
    a. Identify variances between amounts capitalized each month and the capital budget.
    b. Analyze a sample of capital transactions each quarter to detect instances in which installed material was transferred to inventory.
    c. Review all journal entries that transferred costs from capital to inventory accounts.
    d. Compare inventory receipts with debits to the inventory account and investigate discrepancies.

64. An audit of an organization's claims department determined that a large number of duplicate payments had been issued due to problems in the claims processing system. During the exit conference, the vice president of the claims department informed the auditors that attempts to recover the duplicate payments would be initiated immediately and that the claims processing system would be enhanced within six months to correct the problems. Based on this response, the chief audit executive should:
    a. Adjust the scope of the next regularly scheduled audit of the claims department to assess controls within the claims processing system.
    b. Monitor the status of corrective action and schedule a follow-up engagement when appropriate.
    c. Schedule a follow-up engagement within six months to assess the status of corrective action.
    d. Discuss the findings with the audit committee and ask the committee to determine the appropriate follow-up action.

65. As part of a manufacturing company's environmental, health, and safety (EHS) self-inspection program, inspections are conducted by a member of the EHS staff and the operational manager for a given work area or building. If a deficiency cannot be immediately corrected, the EHS staff member enters it into a tracking database that is accessible to all departments via a local area network. The EHS manager uses the database to provide senior management with quarterly activity reports regarding corrective action. During review of the self-inspection program, an auditor notes that the operational manager enters the closure information and affirms that corrective action is complete. What change in the control system would compensate for this potential conflict of interest?
    a. No additional control is needed because the quarterly report is reviewed by senior management, providing adequate oversight in this situation.
    b. No additional control is needed because those implementing a corrective action are in the best position to evaluate the adequacy and completion of that action.
    c. After closure is entered into the system, review by the EHS staff member of the original inspection team should be required in order to verify closure.
    d. The EHS department secretary should be responsible for entering all information in the tracking system based on memos from the operational manager.

66. Which of the following statements best describes the internal audit function's responsibility for follow-up activities related to a previous engagement?
    a. Internal auditors should determine if corrective action has been taken and is achieving the desired results or if management has assumed the risk of not taking the corrective action.
    b. Internal auditors should determine if management has initiated corrective action, but they have no responsibility to determine if the action is achieving the desired results. That determination is management's responsibility.
    c. The chief audit executive is responsible for scheduling follow-up activities only if directed to do so by senior management or the audit committee. Otherwise, follow-up is entirely discretionary.
    d. None of the above.

67. Which of the following describes the most appropriate action to be taken concerning a repeated observation of violations of company policy pertaining to competitive bidding?
    a. The engagement final communication should note that this same condition had been reported in the prior engagement.
    b. During the exit interview, management should be made aware that the violation has not been corrected.
    c. The chief audit executive should determine whether management or the board has assumed the risk of not taking corrective action.
    d. The chief audit executive should determine whether this condition should be reported to the external auditor and any regulatory agency.

68. When conducting audit follow-up of a finding related to cash management routines, which of the following does **not** need to be considered?
    a. Inherent risk has been eliminated as a result of resolution of the condition.
    b. The steps being taken are resolving the condition disclosed by the finding.
    c. Controls have been implemented to deter or detect a recurrence of the finding.
    d. Benefits have accrued to the entity as a result of resolving the condition.

69. A follow-up review found that a significant internal control weakness had not been corrected. The chief audit executive (CAE) discussed this matter with senior management and was informed of management's willingness to accept the risk. The CAE should:
    a. Do nothing further because management is responsible for deciding the appropriate action to be taken in response to reported engagement observations and recommendations.
    b. Initiate a fraud investigation to determine if employees had taken advantage of the internal control weakness.
    c. Inform senior management that the weakness must be corrected and schedule another follow-up review.
    d. Assess the reasons that senior management decided to accept the risk and inform the board of senior management's decision.

70. An audit committee is concerned that management is not addressing all internal audit observations and recommendations. What should the audit committee do to address this situation?
    a. Require managers to provide detailed action plans with specific dates for addressing audit observations and recommendations.
    b. Require all managers to confirm when they have taken action.
    c. Require the chief executive officer to report why action has not been taken.
    d. Require the chief audit executive to establish procedures to monitor progress.

71. Questions used to interrogate individuals suspected of fraud should:
    a. Adhere to a predetermined order.
    b. Cover more than one subject or topic.
    c. Move from the general to the specific.
    d. Direct the individual to a desired answer.

72. An auditor for a major retail company suspects that inventory fraud is occurring at three stores that have high cost of goods sold. Which of the following audit activities would provide the most persuasive evidence that fraud is occurring?
    a. Use an integrated test facility (ITF) to compare individual sales transactions with test transactions submitted through the ITF. Investigate all differences.
    b. Interview the three individual store managers to determine if their explanations about the observed differences are the same, and then compare their explanations to that of the section manager.
    c. Schedule a surprise inventory audit to include a physical inventory. Investigate areas of inventory shrinkage.
    d. Select a sample of individual store prices and compare them with the sales entered on the cash register for the same items.

73. A chief audit executive (CAE) suspects that several employees have used desktop computers for personal gain. In conducting an investigation, the primary reason that the CAE chose to engage a forensic information systems auditor rather than using the organization's information systems auditor is that a forensic information systems auditor would possess:
    a. Knowledge of the computing system that would enable a more comprehensive assessment of the computer use and abuse.
    b. Knowledge of what constitutes evidence acceptable in a court of law.
    c. Superior analytical skills that would facilitate the identification of computer abuse.
    d. Superior documentation and organization skills that would facilitate in the presentation of findings to senior management and the board.

74. If an internal auditor is interviewing three individuals, one of whom is suspected of committing a fraud, which of the following is the **least** effective approach?
    a. Ask each individual to prepare a written statement explaining his or her actions.
    b. Take the role of one seeking the truth.
    c. Listen carefully to what each interviewee has to say.
    d. Attempt to get the suspected individual to confess.

75. Which of the following is most likely to be considered an indication of possible fraud?
    a. The replacement of the management team after a hostile takeover.
    b. Rapid turnover of the organization's financial executives.
    c. Rapid expansion into new markets.
    d. A government audit of the organization's tax returns.

76. What computer-assisted audit technique would an auditor use to identify a fictitious or terminated employee?
    a. Parallel simulation of payroll calculations.
    b. Exception testing for payroll deductions.
    c. Recalculations of net pay.
    d. Tagging and tracing of payroll tax-rate changes.

77. Which of the following would **not** be considered a condition that indicates a higher likelihood of fraud?
    a. Management has delegated the authority to make purchases under a certain dollar limit to subordinates.
    b. An individual has held the same cash-handling job for an extended period without any rotation of duties.
    c. An individual handling marketable securities is responsible for making the purchases, recording the purchases, and reporting any discrepancies and gains or losses to senior management.
    d. The assignment of responsibility and accountability in the accounts receivable department is not clear.

78. The most common motivation for management fraud is the existence of:
    a. Vices, such as a gambling habit.
    b. Job dissatisfaction.
    c. Financial pressures on the organization.
    d. The challenge of committing the perfect crime.

79. Which of the following would indicate that fraud may be taking place in a marketing department?
    a. There is no documentation for some fairly large expenditures made to a new vendor.
    b. A manager appears to be living a lifestyle that is in excess of what could be provided by a marketing manager's salary.
    c. The control environment can best be described as "very loose." However, this attitude is justified by management on the grounds that it is needed for creativity.
    d. All of the above.

80. Which sampling plan requires no additional sampling once the first error is found?
    a. Stratified sampling.
    b. Attributes sampling.
    c. Stop-or-go sampling.
    d. Discovery sampling

81. A bank internal auditor wishes to determine whether all loans are supported by sufficient collateral, properly aged regarding current payments, and accurately categorized as current or noncurrent. The best audit procedure to accomplish these objectives would be to:
    a. Use generalized audit software to read the total loan file, age the file by last payment due, and extract a statistical sample stratified by the current and aged population. Examine each loan selected for proper collateralization and aging.
    b. Select a block sample of all loans in excess of a specified dollar limit and determine if they are current and properly categorized. For each loan approved, verify aging and categorization.
    c. Select a discovery sample of all loan applications to determine whether each application contains a statement of collateral.
    d. Select a sample of payments made on the loan portfolio and trace them to loans to see if the payments are properly applied. For each loan identified, examine the loan application to determine that the loan has proper collateralization.

82. An important difference between a statistical and a judgmental sample is that with a statistical sample:
    a. No judgment is required because everything is computed according to a formula.
    b. A smaller sample can be used.
    c. More accurate results are obtained.
    d. Population estimates with measurable reliability can be made.

83. Variability of the dollar amount of individual items in a population affects sample size in which of the following sampling plans?
    a. Attributes sampling.
    b. Dollar-unit sampling.
    c. Mean-per-unit sampling.
    d. Discovery sampling.

84. The following X-bar chart is an example of the output from a computer application used by a health insurance company to monitor physician bill amounts for various surgical procedures:

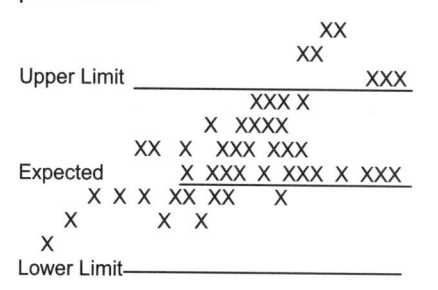

    ```
                                    XX
                                    XX
    Upper Limit _____ XXX
                                 XXX X
                              X  XXXX
                           XX X   XXX XXX
    Expected               X XXX X XXX X XXX
                        X X X  XX XX    X
                     X          X  X
                  X
    Lower Limit_____
    ```

    The data plotted on the chart represents:
    a. Random variation.
    b. Abnormal variation.
    c. Normal variation.
    d. Cyclic variation.

85. The standard error of a sample reflects:
    a. The projected population error based on errors in the sample.
    b. The average rate of error in the sample.
    c. The degree of variation in sample items.
    d. The error in the population that the auditor can accept.

86. An auditor is conducting a survey of perceptions and beliefs of employees concerning an organization's health-care plan. The best approach to selecting a sample would be to:
    a. Focus on people who are likely to respond so that a larger sample can be obtained.
    b. Focus on managers and supervisors because they can also reflect the opinions of the people in their departments.
    c. Use stratified sampling where the strata are defined by marital and family status, age, and salaried or hourly status.
    d. Use monetary-unit sampling according to employee salaries.

87. Which of the following is **not** an advantage of sending an internal control questionnaire prior to an audit engagement?
    a. The engagement client can use the questionnaire for self-evaluation prior to the auditor's visit.
    b. The questionnaire will help the engagement client understand the scope of the engagement.
    c. Preparing the questionnaire will help the auditor plan the scope of the engagement and organize the information to be gathered.
    d. The engagement client will respond only to the questions asked, without volunteering additional information.

88. Which of the following techniques could be used to estimate the standard deviation for a sampling plan?
    a. Ratio estimation.
    b. Pilot sample.
    c. Regression.
    d. Discovery sampling.

89. As used in the verification of an accounts payable schedule, which of the following is best described as an analytical test?
    a. Comparing the items on the schedule with the accounts payable ledger or unpaid voucher file.
    b. Comparing the balance on the schedule with the balances of prior years.
    c. Comparing confirmations received from selected creditors with the accounts payable ledger.
    d. Examining vendors' invoices in support of selected items on the schedule.

90. The use of an analytical review to verify the correctness of various operating expenses would **not** be a preferred approach if:
    a. An auditor notes strong indicators of a specific fraud involving these accounts.
    b. Operations are relatively stable and have not changed much over the past year.
    c. An auditor would like to identify large, unusual, or non-recurring transactions during the year.
    d. Operating expenses vary in relation to other operating expenses, but not in relation to revenue.

91. Which of the following analytical review procedures should an auditor use to determine if a change in investment income during the current year was due to changes in investment strategy, changes in portfolio mix, or other factors?
    a. Simple linear regression of investment income changes over the past five years to determine the nature of the changes.
    b. Ratio analysis of changes in the investment portfolio on a monthly basis.
    c. Trend analysis of changes in investment income as a percentage of total assets and of investment assets over the past five years.
    d. Multiple regression analysis using independent variables related to the nature of the investment portfolio and market conditions.

92. Which of the following procedures would provide the best evidence of the effectiveness of a credit-granting function?
    a. Observe the process.
    b. Review the trend in receivables write-offs.
    c. Ask the credit manager about the effectiveness of the function.
    d. Check for evidence of credit approval on a sample of customer orders.

93. A production manager ordered excessive raw materials for delivery to a separate company owned by the manager. The manager falsified receiving documents and approved the invoices for payment. Which of the following audit procedures would most likely detect this fraud?
    a. Select a sample of cash disbursements and compare purchase orders, receiving reports, invoices, and check copies.
    b. Select a sample of cash disbursements and confirm the amount purchased, purchase price, and date of shipment with the vendors.
    c. Observe the receiving dock and count materials received; compare the counts to receiving reports completed by receiving personnel.
    d. Perform analytical tests, comparing production, materials purchased, and raw materials inventory levels; investigate differences.

94. When using a rational decision-making process, the next step after definition of the problem is:
    a. Developing alternative solutions.
    b. Identifying acceptable levels of risk.
    c. Recognizing the gap between reality and expectations.
    d. Confirming hypotheses.

95. A flowchart of process activities and controls may provide:
    a. Information on where fraud could occur.
    b. Information on the extent of a past fraud.
    c. An indication of where fraud has occurred in a process.
    d. No information related to fraud prevention.

96. Which of the following factors is **least** essential to a successful control self-assessment workshop?
    a. Voting technology.
    b. Facilitation training.
    c. Prior planning.
    d. Group dynamics.

97. A manufacturer uses a materials requirements planning (MRP) system to track inventory, orders, and raw material requirements. A preliminary audit assessment indicates that the organization's inventory is understated. Using audit software, what conditions should the auditor search for in the MRP database to support this hypothesis?

    I. Item cost set at zero.
    II. Negative quantities on hand.
    III. Order quantity exceeding requirements.
    IV. Inventory lead times exceeding delivery schedule.

    a. I and II only.
    b. I and IV only.
    c. II and IV only.
    d. III and IV only.

98. An organization provides credit cards to selected employees for business use. The credit card company provides a computer file of all transactions by employees of the organization. An auditor plans to use generalized audit software to select relevant transactions for testing. Which of the following would **not** be readily identified using generalized audit software?
    a. High-dollar transactions.
    b. Fraudulent transactions.
    c. Transactions for specific cardholders.
    d. Suppliers used by each cardholder.

99. Internal auditors often flowchart a control system and reference the flowchart to narrative descriptions of certain activities. This is an appropriate procedure to:
    a. Determine whether the system meets established management objectives.
    b. Document that the system meets international auditing requirements.
    c. Determine whether the system can be relied upon to produce accurate information.
    d. Gain the understanding necessary to test the effectiveness of the system.

100. Compared to a vertical flowchart, which of the following is true of a horizontal flowchart?
    a. It provides more room for written descriptions that parallel the symbols.
    b. It brings into sharper focus the assignment of duties and independent checks on performance.
    c. It is usually longer.
    d. It does not cross departmental lines.

END OF PART II QUESTIONS

PLEASE NOTE: The actual CIA exam Part II will contain **125 exam questions**. The 125 questions will include up to 25 unscored questions, which will be used for research purposes. These unscored questions will be interspersed with the scored questions and will not be identified as unscored questions. Candidates should therefore answer all 125 questions to the best of their ability.

Solutions for Part II – Conducting the Internal Audit Engagement

The solutions and suggested explanations for Part II of the Certified Internal Auditor Model Exam Questions are provided on the following pages.

The chart below cross-references the question numbers for Part II with the topics tested:

Topic Tested	Question Number
Conduct Engagements	1 – 31
Conduct Specific Engagements	32 – 61
Monitor Engagement Outcomes	62 – 70
Fraud Knowledge Elements	71 – 80
Engagement Tools	81 – 100

1. **Solution: b (I and IV only)**
   I. Correct. According to Implementation Standard 2110.A2: "The internal audit activity should evaluate risk exposures relating to the organization's governance, operations, and information systems regarding the:
      - Reliability and integrity of financial and operational information.
      - Effectiveness and efficiency of operations.
      - Safeguarding of assets.
      - Compliance with laws, regulations, and contracts."

      The specific engagement objective of determining if goods are charged to the appropriate account would address the objective regarding the reliability and integrity of information.
   II. Incorrect. The specific engagement objective described does not address compliance.
   III. Incorrect. The specific engagement objective described may address effectiveness of operations but does not address efficiency.
   IV. Correct. The specific engagement objective of determining if all goods paid for have been received would address the objective regarding safeguarding of assets.

2. **Solution: a**
   a. Correct. Auditors must exhibit loyalty to the organization, but must not be a party to any illegal activity. Thus, auditors must comply with legal subpoenas.
   b. Incorrect. Rule of Conduct 3.2 prohibits auditors from using audit information for personal gain.
   c. Incorrect. Rule of Conduct 2.2 prohibits auditors form accepting anything which might be presumed to impair the auditor's professional judgment.
   d. Incorrect. Rule of Conduct 1.3 prohibits auditors from knowingly being a party to any illegal or improper activity. Practice Advisory 1210.A2-1.10 states that significant observations of illegal activity should be reported to the audit committee.

3. **Solution: b**
   a. Incorrect. The auditor must act consistently with the spirit embodied in the *IIA Code of Ethics*. It would not be practical to seek the advice of legal counsel for all ethical decisions. Ethics is a moral and professional concept, not just a legal concept.
   b. Correct. This is consistent with the concepts embodied in the *IIA Code of Ethics*.
   c. Incorrect. It would not be practical to seek the audit committee's advice for all potential dilemmas. Further, the advice might not be consistent with the profession's standards.
   d. Incorrect. If the company's standards are not consistent with, or as high as, the profession's standards, the professional internal auditor should abide by the standards of the profession.

4. **Solution: b**
   a. Incorrect. The auditor has sufficient evidence to bring the matter to the attention of management and let them decide the method of further investigation.
   b. Correct. This is the correct answer according to Practice Advisory 1210.A2-1.6.
   c. Incorrect. There is no need to inform divisional management of the audit suspicions. It would be appropriate to interview divisional management, but primarily for data gathering purposes.
   d. Incorrect. The auditor's responsibility is for reporting inside the organization.

5. **Solution: b**
   a. Incorrect. The activities described must be performed before the fieldwork can be undertaken.
   b. Correct. These activities are normally accomplished during the preliminary survey phase.
   c. Incorrect. The activities described must be performed before the engagement program can be developed.
   d. Incorrect. The activities described must be performed before the evidence can be examined or evaluated.

6. **Solution: a**
    a. Correct. This is the appropriate action according to Practice Advisory 1210.A2-1.13.
    b. Incorrect. The auditor should first expand work to determine the existence of fraud before reporting the matter to senior management. At this point, the auditor only has suspicions of fraud, given the red flags. More work should be performed before consulting with management, external legal counsel, or the audit committee.
    c. Incorrect. See answer "b".
    d. Incorrect. See answer "b".

7. **Solution: d**
    a. Incorrect. Although these statistics might not be quite as relevant as some of the other choices of data sets, the data would have great validity, having been compiled and published by an independent source.
    b. Incorrect. The dollar amounts in this group of data would be objective and valid, representing the actual experiences of the organization.
    c. Incorrect. These amounts would include cash as well as credit sales, and the inclusion of the cash sales would reduce the relevance of these data to the model. However, these dollar amounts in this group of data also represent the actual experiences of the organization and thus have a high degree of validity.
    d. Correct. Opinion evidence does not have as much validity as factual evidence. In addition, the source of the evidence may have a bias, which should be considered by the internal auditor when evaluating the validity of this data.

8. **Solution: d**
    a. Incorrect. This is a mechanical aspect of evidence; it has no specific relationship to any of the characteristics of evidence.
    b. Incorrect. This is a quality of competence of evidence.
    c. Incorrect. This is a quality of relevance of evidence.
    d. Correct. This is one of the qualities of sufficiency of evidence.

9. **Solution: a**
    a. Correct. This information is generated by external parties and does not pass through the operations of the audited area and therefore has the greatest evidentiary weight.
    b. Incorrect. This is considered internal-external information, which is initiated by the audited area and is subject to distortion.
    c. Incorrect. This is considered internal information, generated by the audited area, which is subject to distortion.
    d. Incorrect. This is considered external-internal information. Although it is initiated externally, it is maintained by the audited area and can therefore be distorted.

10. **Solution: a**
    a. Correct. Competent evidence is reliable evidence and the best attainable through the use of appropriate audit techniques.
    b. Incorrect. This is the definition of physical evidence. All physical evidence is not necessarily competent; in fact, the quality of competence is more often associated with documentary evidence.
    c. Incorrect. This is the definition of corroborative evidence. While corroborative evidence may be competent, much competent evidence is primary rather than supplementary.
    d. Incorrect. This is the definition of circumstantial evidence. Circumstantial evidence is not necessarily competent evidence.

11. **Solution: a**
    a. Correct. A confirmation from a customer is the most reliable evidence that a receivable exists.
    b. Incorrect. An invoice is not particularly reliable because it is not developed external to the company and does not consider subsequent payment.
    c. Incorrect. This is not evidence of a receivable.
    d. Incorrect. This is not as reliable as a confirmation, and it does not confirm the continued existence of the receivable.

12. **Solution: d**
    a. Incorrect. Fictitious sales would be a plausible answer since they would generate additional uncollectible accounts receivable that are not necessarily being reflected in the allowance for bad debts.
    b. Incorrect. Ineffective credit and collection procedures would be a plausible answer since they could contribute to increases in uncollectible accounts receivable that are not necessarily being reflected in the allowance for bad debts.
    c. Incorrect. An understated allowance for bad debts would be a plausible answer since it would contribute to overstatements in net accounts receivable and decreases in the accounts receivable turnover ratio.
    d. Correct. Overstated sales returns for credit would not be a plausible answer since they would understate (not overstate) accounts receivable. This would result in especially lower (not higher) net accounts receivable balances as a percentage of total assets.

13. **Solution: b**
    a. Incorrect. This should have the opposite effect.
    b. Correct. With a liberal credit policy, customers would be taking longer to pay (365/4.3 compared to 365/7.3).
    c. Incorrect. This should have the opposite effect.
    d. Incorrect. This is irrelevant, since cash sales will have no impact.

14. **Solution: a**
    a. Correct. Only a category such as new employee would generate a payroll change.
    b. Incorrect. The computer calculates this. It is not a change and would not be on the list.
    c. Incorrect. This data should come from the time reporting system (time card or time sheet). It is not a payroll change.
    d. Incorrect. This is not applicable to a listing of payroll changes.

15. **Solution: c**
    a. Incorrect. The scattergram does not show a relationship between training costs and sales revenue.
    b. Incorrect. The scattergram does not yield information about the effectiveness of the training program.
    c. Correct. The scattergram suggests that training costs and sales revenue are not related.
    d. Incorrect. There is nothing to indicate an incorrect data point in this graph.

16. **Solution: d (I, II, and III)**
    I, II, III. Correct. All workpapers should contain pertinent information to support observations and recommendations.

17. **Solution: a**
    a. Correct. By tying groups of workpapers together, summaries provide an orderly and logical flow and facilitate supervisory review.
    b. Incorrect. Summaries are part of the workpaper file, not a replacement.
    c. Incorrect. Senior management is either given the entire report or provided with an executive summary or digest of the report contents. Workpaper summaries would not be appropriate for senior management.
    d. Incorrect. Engagement observations are developed using the attributes of an observation. See Practice Advisory 2410-1.6 and 7.

18. **Solution: b (I, II, and III only)**
    I, II, III. Correct. The *Professional Practices Framework* specifies that I, II, and III are acceptable approaches for documenting supervisory review of engagement workpapers.
    IV. Incorrect. Although performance appraisals might mention reviews of workpapers, they do not represent sufficient evidence of review.

19. **Solution: c**
    a. Incorrect. This answer is incomplete because it ignores facts (evidence) and recommendations.
    b. Incorrect. This answer is incomplete because it ignores evidence and recommendations.
    c. Correct. This is the most complete of the choices.
    d. Incorrect. This answer is incomplete because it ignores evidence, objectives, conclusions, and recommendations.

20. **Solution: d**
    a. Incorrect. There is no need for earlier consideration in this situation.
    b. Incorrect. Changes in auditor methodology are not of particular importance to the engagement client.
    c. Incorrect. Indications of possible fraud would not be communicated to the engagement client.
    d. Correct. Such a situation would require immediate attention.

21. **Solution: c**
    a. Incorrect. The actual number of meters replaced is less than the goal; therefore, the goal is not being met.
    b. Incorrect. Corrective action has apparently not been taken since actual replacements did not meet the goal.
    c. Correct. The goal has not been met and corrective action is needed. According to Practice Advisory 2100-1.1, internal auditors are involved in evaluating and improving the effectiveness of control. Determining whether deviations from operating standards are identified, analyzed, and communicated to those responsible for corrective action is one way of accomplishing this function.
    d. Incorrect. This cannot be determined from the information given.

22. **Solution: a**
    a. Correct. The same number of reported leaks are being repaired. The established goal is being met. Implementation Standard 2120.A3 states that internal auditors should review operations and programs to ascertain the extent to which results are consistent with established goals and objectives to determine whether operations and programs are being implemented or performed as intended.
    b. Incorrect. There are no deviations from the goal.
    c. Incorrect. The operating standard should not be changed since there is no problem meeting the standard and the standard cannot be higher than the number of leaks reported.
    d. Incorrect. Staffing cannot be evaluated based on the information provided.

23. **Solution: b**
    a. Incorrect. The actual unmetered water percentage is greater than the goal; therefore, the goal was not met.
    b. Correct. Practice Advisory 2320-1.3 states that analytical auditing procedures assist internal auditors in identifying conditions, which may require subsequent engagement procedures. Since month three is at standard, the deviation in month two was probably corrected so further audit work is not warranted.
    c. Incorrect. The deviation in month two was apparently corrected.
    d. Incorrect. There is no evidence that the operating standard is inappropriate.

24. **Solution: a**
    a. Correct. Without knowledge of guidelines for compliance, a reasonable conclusion cannot be reached.
    b. Incorrect. The fact that no minority has been hired this year is irrelevant without knowing the total hires for the period.
    c. Incorrect. An affirmative-action policy is clearly auditable.
    d. Incorrect. This conclusion cannot be reached without knowledge of the actual company policy.

25. **Solution: a**
    a. Correct. Recommendations represent options that are available to management.
    b. Incorrect. Problems must be resolved in the manner deemed appropriate by management, not the auditor.
    c. Incorrect. Providing recommendations may enable management to reduce the costs/time of addressing audit findings, but there is no guarantee of this.
    d. Incorrect. See answer "c".

26. **Solution: c (II, III, and IV only)**
    II, III, IV. Correct. Practice Advisory 2410-1.1 states that engagement final communications should contain, at a minimum, the purpose, scope, and results of the engagement.
    I, V. Incorrect. Background information and summaries are not required elements of an engagement final communication.

27. **Solution: c**
    a. Incorrect. Resolving conflicts is an objective of the exit conference.
    b. Incorrect. Discussing the engagement observations in order to reach agreement on the facts is an objective of the exit conference.
    c. Correct. Identifying concerns for future engagements is not a primary objective of the exit conference.
    d. Incorrect. Determining management's action plan and responses is an objective of the exit conference.

28. **Solution: c**
    a. Incorrect. The procedures do not represent a deficiency since efficiency has improved without diminishing control.
    b. Incorrect. A flowchart is not the best form of documentation because it does not address efficiency.
    c. Correct. This represents a change in process that should be brought to the attention of management and documented.
    d. Incorrect. The engagement should be completed.

29. **Solution: d**
   a. Incorrect. An engagement client should have an opportunity to respond before the report is written.
   b. Incorrect. Internal auditors make recommendations; they do not submit requirements.
   c. Incorrect. Where appropriate, external auditors would review workpapers to accomplish this end.
   d. Correct. Audit reports should present the purpose, scope, and results of an engagement.

30. **Solution: d**
   a. Incorrect. Requests for feedback from customers is best achieved by the customer completing a questionnaire designed for the purpose. Such questionnaires facilitate the development of useful quality performance measures and trends.
   b. Incorrect. See answer "a".
   c. Incorrect. The questionnaire should be given to the customer at the beginning of the engagement for completion after the engagement. Distributing questionnaires long after the engagement is completed would be less useful because the information will not be fresh in the customer's mind.
   d. Correct. It is best practice to provide the questionnaire to the customer at the beginning of an engagement, either routinely or periodically, to complete after the engagement. The quality measures being used by the internal audit activity and the internal auditor are then clearly understood by the customer, and specific requirements and expectations can be noted by the internal auditor before the engagement begins. The customer can then assess the quality of the internal audit work during the engagement, and complete the questionnaire after the engagement. This also encourages a continuous process of monitoring quality and feedback by the customer throughout the engagement.

31. **Solution: c**
   a. Incorrect. In a performance appraisal of a below-average performer, it is appropriate and advisable to notify the employee of the upcoming appraisal, use objective language, and document the appraisal.
   b. Incorrect. See answer "a".
   c. Correct. It is not appropriate to use generalizations when giving a performance appraisal to a below-average performer. Rather, the evaluator must cite specific information and be prepared to support assertions with evidence.
   d. Incorrect. See answer "a".

32. **Solution: a**
   a. Correct. Controls at the service bureau and the user organization are both important to the controls of the overall payroll function.
   b. Incorrect. The internal controls at the information service bureau and the user organization interact with each other, so both must be reviewed.
   c. Incorrect. This would change the scope of the engagement.
   d. Incorrect. Though the processing is being performed outside the organization, the external information service bureau is an extension of the organization's information systems. In fact, the risk may be higher since an external organization controls part of the internal control environment. Also, the recent change increases the company's risk, as does the complexity of communicating between the organization and the service bureau.

33. **Solution: d**
   a. Incorrect. This is a management decision.
   b. Incorrect. This is a management responsibility.
   c. Incorrect. The chief audit executive should report the violation to senior management or the board before scheduling any audit activity.
   d. Correct. Upon the discovery of fraud or unethical conduct, the chief audit executive should inform executive management and the audit committee.

34. **Solution: d**
    a. Incorrect. This would be an effective procedure because it would prevent the addition of a fictitious company to the authorized vendor list.
    b. Incorrect. This would be effective because a vendor would not be paid if parts were not used in actual production.
    c. Incorrect. This would also be effective because it would ensure that all vendors are authorized.
    d. Correct. This would be the least effective because it controls the total amount of expenditures, but does not control where the purchase orders are placed or whether there is receipt of goods for the items purchased.

35. **Solution: c**
    a. Incorrect. The interviewee may be less likely to confess or provide other useful information if the supervisor is present.
    b. Incorrect. The interview should take place in a room that allows privacy, but there should be no physical barriers, including a locked door, to prevent the suspect from leaving if he or she wishes.
    c. Correct. Wording choices, such as shifts in the use of pronouns and verbs, may indicate areas of dishonesty or fabrication.
    d. Incorrect. During an admission-seeking interview, the interviewer should appear confident that the suspect committed the fraud. Therefore, the interviewer should ask how, not if, the interviewee committed the fraud.

36. **Solution: b**
    a. Incorrect. This phrase best describes a process-based approach, although control processes are not the only processes reviewed in this approach.
    b. Correct. A control-based approach concentrates on how well controls are working to manage risks. The key risks and controls are generally identified before the workshop.
    c. Incorrect. While control design could be compared to control frameworks in a control-based approach, this does not adequately describe the process. A control-based process is more likely to examine the gap between control design and control effectiveness in managing risks.
    d. Incorrect. Cost-effectiveness could be discussed in a control-based control self-assessment workshop, but it is not the primary focus of this process.

37. **Solution: d**
    a. Incorrect. Program audit engagements address accomplishment of program objectives.
    b. Incorrect. Financial auditing addresses accuracy of financial records.
    c. Incorrect. Compliance auditing addresses compliance with requirements, including legal and regulatory requirements.
    d. Correct. Operational auditing is most likely to address a determination of cost savings by focusing on economy and efficiency.

38. **Solution: d**
    a. Incorrect. Validity and reliability of each question is extremely important.
    b. Incorrect. See answer "a".
    c. Incorrect. When questionnaires are too long, people tend not to complete them.
    d. Correct. Questions can be multiple-choice, fill-in-the-blank, essay, Likert scales, etc.

39. **Solution: c**
    a. Incorrect. Financial audit engagements involve review of financial information.
    b. Incorrect. Compliance audit engagements involve examining control procedures and there compliance.
    c. Correct. Performance audit engagements involve review of performance against set criteria.
    d. Incorrect. Operational audit engagements involve reviewing organizational and departmental structures.

40. **Solution: c**
    a. Incorrect. This procedure is designed to identify payments for liabilities not included in the prior period, but paid in the subsequent period.
    b. Incorrect. This procedure is designed to identify amounts not included in the accounts payable. Zero balance accounts should be verified as part of the process.
    c. Correct. This procedure provides no evidence pertaining to unrecorded liabilities.
    d. Incorrect. Tracing receiving reports from before the period end to invoices and the payables listing is designed to assure that these shipments are included in the payables.

41. **Solution: d**
    a. Incorrect. Diversifying risk is a frequent reason for a company to merge with or acquire another company.
    b. Incorrect. Responding to government policy is a frequent reason for a company to merge with or acquire another company.
    c. Incorrect. Reducing labor costs is a frequent reason for a company to merge with or acquire another company.
    d. Correct. Increasing stock prices is not a frequent reason for a company to merge with or acquire another company because this effect could be achieved through other methods that directly benefit company performance.

42. **Solution: c (I and II only)**
    I. Correct. This addresses the propriety of costs as a result of the change orders.
    II. Correct. This addresses the accuracy of costs resulting from the change orders.
    III. Incorrect. This procedure tests whether the company agreed to the work done by the contractor but does not test whether the contractor properly accounted for the costs related to the work.

43. **Solution: a**
    a. Correct. The logical starting point is to determine the point(s) of control. Evidence of license compliance can then be assessed.
    b. Incorrect. Before taking this step, an auditor would first determine if installation is controlled centrally because this would affect how the auditor would ascertain information on the installed software.
    c. Incorrect. This would help an auditor determine if software was legitimately purchased but the auditor would still need to start by determining where the software is installed, and answer "a" would be a more useful starting point.
    d. Incorrect. Monitoring usage would not be as important as determining installation processes when evaluating license compliance.

44. **Solution: a**
    a. Correct. Verifying is the most often used technique in testing the accuracy of information maintained by a system, whether manual or automated.
    b. Incorrect. Testing the program will not test the accuracy of data in the database.
    c. Incorrect. Simulating normal processing would test the program but not the accuracy of data.
    d. Incorrect. Tracing would require that additional coding be inserted into the database system programs.

45. **Solution: a**
    a. Correct. A feasibility study should be conducted in the systems analysis stage.
    b. Incorrect. The involvement of users in the development process at various points is important.
    c. Incorrect. This ensures the quality in the development process at various points.
    d. Incorrect. Without good documentation, an information system may be difficult, if not impossible, to operate, maintain, or use.

46. **Solution: c**
    a. Incorrect. Competitors' processing may be irrelevant or totally unknown.
    b. Incorrect. Emphasis should first be on the purposes and needs of the new system, not on equipment.
    c. Correct. Users' information needs and objectives should be primary.
    d. Incorrect. Controls related to the old (current) system may be irrelevant or unimportant.

47. **Solution: c**
    a. Incorrect. Use of scripts is a common practice to sequence events.
    b. Incorrect. Recovery contracts are not updated that frequently.
    c. Correct. Failure to store backup media off-site is a very serious control weakness.
    d. Incorrect. Generally, the limited test-time window will only permit testing a few systems.

48. **Solution: b (I and IV only)**
    I, IV. Correct. These tests can identify duplicate payments.
    II, III. Incorrect. Selection of transactions with unauthorized vendor codes and testing of transactions for reasonableness do not identify duplicate payments.

49. **Solution: d**
    a. Incorrect. Comparison with industry standards will not test the accuracy of internal reporting.
    b. Incorrect. Comparison with industry standards will not test the controls designed to safeguard the inventory.
    c. Incorrect. Comparison with industry standards will not test compliance.
    d. Correct. Such an analytical procedure will provide an indication of the efficiency and effectiveness of the subsidiary's management of the inventory.

50. **Solution: b**
    a. Incorrect. This procedure only provides data on whether payments agree with invoices. It does not provide data on whether the invoiced amounts are correct.
    b. Correct. This would help the auditor determine that all three pieces of data were most likely matched before payment.
    c. Incorrect. As with answer "a", this only provides data on whether payments agree with invoices. It does not provide data on whether the goods were actually received.
    d. Incorrect. This provides data only on one day. While it matches items received with those paid, it does not provide data on whether the billings were correct.

51. **Solution: d**
    a. Incorrect. Benchmarking involves a comparison against industry leaders or "world-class" operations. Benchmarking either uses industry-wide figures (to protect the confidentiality of information provided by participating organizations) or figures from cooperating organizations.
    b. Incorrect. Benchmarking requires measurements, which involve quantitative comparisons.
    c. Incorrect. Benchmarking can be applied to all of the functional areas in a company. In fact, because manufacturing often tends to be industry-specific whereas things like processing an order or paying an invoice are not, there is a greater opportunity to improve by learning from global leaders.
    d. Correct. See answer "a".

52. **Solution: a**
    a. Correct. This would be the least effective procedure because: (1) it provides only a comparison with the past period and that past period may have been suffering from the same problem; and (2) it is a global test.
    b. Incorrect. Using an integrated test facility (ITF) would be a very good procedure here because the concern is whether the interest rate calculation is made correctly.
    c. Incorrect. Test data would be very effective because it provides a direct test of the interest rate calculation.
    d. Incorrect. This would be the most effective procedure because the auditor is taking a detailed sample of actual transactions.

53. **Solution: a**
    a. Correct. The internal audit activity should be involved to ensure the existence of performance specifications consistent with the hospital's needs because incomplete or erroneous specifications may result in the acquisition of unusable software or unenforceable contract terms with the software vendor.
    b. Incorrect. The internal audit activity cannot ensure that the application design meets internal development and documentation standards because an external group with different standards has already developed the system.
    c. Incorrect. There is no prototype in procurement of proprietary software.
    d. Incorrect. For externally developed systems, the only omitted or abbreviated systems development life cycle step is programming of the actual system. All other phases remain, even if they are modified.

54. **Solution: a**
    a. Correct. Such training should be planned and is of a continuous nature. It should be subject to a consulting agreement that is formal and written to ensure that the needs and expectations of those that will be trained are recognized and satisfied.
    b. Incorrect. This type of agreement applies more to routine tasks.
    c. Incorrect. This type of agreement applies more to occasional, one time special arrangements.
    d. Incorrect. This type of agreement applies more to unplanned engagements.

55. **Solution: c**
    a. Incorrect. Designing systems is presumed to impair audit objectivity.
    b. Incorrect. Drafting procedures for systems is presumed to impair independence.
    c. Correct. According to Practice Advisory 1130.A1-1.4, reviewing systems, even before implementation, is an activity appropriately performed by the internal audit function and does not impair objectivity.
    d. Incorrect. Installing systems of controls is presumed to impair independence.

56. **Solution: c**
    a. Incorrect. Flowcharts are most appropriate for studying internal control design. The audit objective is whether the controls are in place and effective, which indicates the need for a test of controls.
    b. Incorrect. System narratives are most appropriate for studying internal control design. The audit objective is whether the controls are in place and effective, which indicates the need for a test of controls.
    c. Correct. Tests of controls, also known as compliance tests, help an auditor determine whether controls are being followed and are effective. For instance, a policy may require that all large transactions be approved by a manager. As a test of controls, the auditor may sample large transactions and review whether manager approval was obtained and whether the proposed transaction meets all the criteria that the manager was supposed to verify.
    d. Incorrect. Substantive tests are tests to determine whether an objective has been achieved and do not necessarily test internal controls.

57. Solution: a
   a. Correct. Innovations in the production of goods or services do not typically lend themselves to ongoing performance measurement.
   b. Incorrect. Key results in market share track changes to the organization's competitive position.
   c. Incorrect. Key results in customer satisfaction help predict future sales.
   d. Incorrect. Key results in employee development help predict the ability to attract and retain good employees.

58. Solution: b
   a. Incorrect. This comparison would help highlight the effectiveness of the promotion in increasing sales.
   b. Correct. There is no indication that cost of the products sold has changed. The challenge is to address the effectiveness of the promotion.
   c. Incorrect. This is the key analysis as it would show the extent of additional revenue versus cost.
   d. Incorrect. This would be helpful because the sales department may have useful information on new customers and repeat purchases.

59. Solution: c
   a. Incorrect. Neither control self-assessment nor performance measurement will address management's objective of controlling costs.
   b. Incorrect. Although benchmarking may have some applicability, it is not the most appropriate tool.
   c. Correct. A business process review (BPR) assesses the performance of administrative and financial processes, such as within procurement and payables. BPR considers process effectiveness and efficiency, including the presence of appropriate controls, to mitigate business risk. Because the objective is to control cellular phone costs, BPR is the appropriate tool to use in this area.
   d. Incorrect. See answer "a".

60. Solution: a
   a. Correct. Comparison against organizations that perform related functions within the same technological area provides information on what is being achieved elsewhere in the new business line.
   b. Incorrect. Comparison against the best competitors focuses on performance in related organizations as a whole and likely includes some activities unrelated to the new business line.
   c. Incorrect. Comparison of processes that are virtually the same regardless of industry (such as document processing) would not be as helpful as comparison of processes that are similar in function.
   d. Incorrect. Comparison against the best within the same organization may be misleading, as it does not provide information on what is being accomplished outside the organization in the new business line.

61. Solution: d
   a. Incorrect. This procedure only considers the rework jobs that require remedial action. Not all rework orders reviewed by the engineer will require remedial action.
   b. Incorrect. This test would be useful for verifying that all rework is recorded in the rework log but provides no evidence that the work was reviewed.
   c. Incorrect. Since this procedure begins with only rework jobs that were reviewed, it would not be useful in finding jobs that were not reviewed.
   d. Correct. The best evidence of all work performed is the set of rework order forms and the best evidence of what was reviewed are the entries in the review log. To determine whether all rework was reviewed, the auditor needs to start with the population of all the rework that was performed (that is, rework order forms) and trace to evidence that it was reviewed (that is, review log).

62. **Solution: d**
    a. Incorrect. Transferring the employees is not necessary and would not resolve the control problem.
    b. Incorrect. This may help detect prior problems but it does not create a control to address future problems.
    c. Incorrect. This would not address the problem because it does not involve the vendor master file.
    d. Correct. This is the only option that will correct the deficiency identified during the audit.

63. **Solution: c**
    a. Incorrect. Variances would not identify costs transferred to inventory.
    b. Incorrect. This would sample from all capital transactions while answer "c" would more specifically address all transfers.
    c. Correct. This would focus on the problem of inappropriate transfers.
    d. Incorrect. There would be no inventory receipts for the transfers, so beginning with inventory receipts would not be an effective method to monitor this situation.

64. **Solution: b**
    a. Incorrect. Because the finding is significant, the internal audit activity should not wait until the next regularly scheduled audit to assess the status of corrective action.
    b. Correct. The internal audit activity should monitor the status of the corrective action. A follow-up engagement should be scheduled when changes to the claims processing system have been sufficiently completed to allow for testing of adequacy and effectiveness.
    c. Incorrect. Although management indicated that the corrections should be completed within six months, this may not be the case. As a result, the internal audit activity should monitor the status of corrective action and schedule a follow-up engagement when it is appropriate.
    d. Incorrect. Although the findings should be discussed with the audit committee because of their significance, the scope and timing of a follow-up engagement should be determined by the chief audit executive based on available information.

65. **Solution: c**
    a. Incorrect. Although senior management can use the report to question why certain corrective actions may be behind schedule, they have no way of knowing whether the corrective actions shown as complete were actually completed.
    b. Incorrect. While the operational managers may in fact be the most knowledgeable about the corrective action, independent verification is preferable.
    c. Correct. If there is a step in the process at which someone independent of the area being inspected can evaluate the adequacy and completeness of corrective action, the potential for closure fraud is minimized.
    d. Incorrect. There is nothing inappropriate about the environmental, health, and safety staff entering the initial inspection results. Having the secretary enter closure data does not improve controls since there is still no independent review. It is also less efficient and timely than having the data entered directly in the field.

66. **Solution: a**
    a. Correct. This is stated in Practice Advisory 2500.A1-1.
    b. Incorrect. This contradicts answer "a" and Practice Advisory 2500.A1-1.
    c. Incorrect. Implementation Standard 2500.A1 states that follow-up action should take place. It is not dependent on directives of either management or the audit committee.
    d. Incorrect. See answer "a".

67. Solution: c
   a. Incorrect. This action is insufficient; see answer "c".
   b. Incorrect. This action is insufficient; see answer "c".
   c. Correct. Management may decide to assume the risk of not correcting a reported condition because of the cost or other considerations.
   d. Incorrect. This action would be inappropriate; see answer "c".

68. Solution: a
   a. Correct. It is appropriate to assess whether steps being taken are resolving the condition, appropriate controls have been implemented, and benefits have accrued to the entity. It is not necessary, however, to ensure that inherent risk has been eliminated. (This could only be accomplished by eliminating the use of cash, which is unrealistic.)
   b. Incorrect. See answer "a".
   c. Incorrect. See answer "a".
   d. Incorrect. See answer "a".

69. Solution: d
   a. Incorrect. See answer "d".
   b. Incorrect. See answer "d".
   c. Incorrect. See answer "d".
   d. Correct. Senior management may decide to accept the risk due to cost or other considerations. The chief audit executive needs to assess senior management's rationale and then inform the board of management's decision.

70. Solution: d
   a. Incorrect. Management are responsible for ensuring action on all internal audit observations and recommendations, but some actions may take time to complete and it is not practical to expect that all will be resolved when an audit committee meets.
   b. Incorrect. See answer "a".
   c. Incorrect. See answer "a".
   d. Correct. The chief audit executive is responsible for establishing appropriate procedures for monitoring the progress by management on all internal audit observations and recommendations. This responsibility should be written into its charter by the audit committee, and progress should be reported at each audit committee meeting.

71. Solution: c
   a. Incorrect. The interviewee's answer may suggest a follow-up question that should be asked before asking the next planned question.
   b. Incorrect. This may be confusing for the respondent.
   c. Correct. General information should be obtained first before details are sought.
   d. Incorrect. The interrogator should avoid leading questions, that is, questions that suggest an answer.

72. Solution: c
   a. Incorrect. The ITF only provides evidence on the correctness of computer processing. It would not be relevant to the hypothesized rationale for the operating data.
   b. Incorrect. Interviews provide a weak form of evidence and would be better if the auditor first has substantive documentary evidence.
   c. Correct. If this type of fraud were occurring, it would result in inventory shrinkage. The surprise inventory count would be an effective audit technique.
   d. Incorrect. The problem would be with inventory shrinkage, not with whether items are appropriately keyed in or scanned in at the cash register.

73. **Solution: b**
    a. Incorrect. The organization's information systems auditor would probably have more knowledge of the organization's computing systems.
    b. Correct. The distinguishing characteristic of forensic auditing is the knowledge needed to testify as an expert witness in a court of law. Although a forensic auditor may possess the other attributes listed, the organization's information systems auditor may also possess these skills or knowledge elements.
    c. Incorrect. A forensic auditor would not necessarily have analytical or organizational skills that are superior to those of the organization's auditor.
    d. Incorrect. See answer "c".

74. **Solution: d**
    a. Incorrect. This is a good interviewing technique to use during a fraud investigation.
    b. Incorrect. See answer "a".
    c. Incorrect. See answer "a".
    d. Correct. The auditor should avoid creating the impression of seeking a confession or a conviction.

75. **Solution: b**
    a. Incorrect. This is not unusual and, in and of itself, is not an indication of possible fraud.
    b. Correct. This is considered a red flag that indicates possible fraud.
    c. Incorrect. This is not unusual and, in and of itself, is not an indication of possible fraud.
    d. Incorrect. This is not unusual and, in and of itself, is not an indication of possible fraud.

76. **Solution: b**
    a. Incorrect. In a parallel simulation, data that were processed by the engagement client's system are reprocessed through the auditor's program to determine if the output obtained matches the output generated by the client's system. This technique might identify problems with the client's processing but would not identify a fictitious or terminated employee.
    b. Correct. This type of computer-assisted audit technique (CAAT) program can identify employees who have no deductions. This is important because fictitious or terminated employees will generally not have any deductions.
    c. Incorrect. A CAAT program can recalculate amounts such as gross pay, net pay, taxes and other deductions, and accumulated or used leave times. These recalculations can help determine if the payroll program is operating correctly or if employee files have been altered, but would not identify a fictitious or terminated employee.
    d. Incorrect. In this type of CAAT program, certain actual transactions are "tagged," and as they proceed through the system, a data file is created that traces the processing through the system and permits an auditor to subsequently review that processing. This would not, however, identify a fictitious or terminated employee.

77. **Solution: a**
    a. Correct. This is an acceptable control procedure which is aimed at limiting risk while promoting efficiency. It is not, by itself, considered a condition that indicates a higher likelihood of fraud.
    b. Incorrect. Lack of rotation of duties or cross-training for sensitive jobs is an identified red flag.
    c. Incorrect. This would be an example of an inappropriate segregation of duties, which is an identified red flag.
    d. Incorrect. This is an identified red flag.

78. **Solution: c**
    a. Incorrect. See answer "c".
    b. Incorrect. See answer "c".
    c. Correct. Management fraud benefits organizations rather than individuals, so the existence of financial pressures is the most common motivation. Management perpetrators attempt to make their financial statements appear more attractive because of the financial pressures of restrictive loan covenants, a poor cash position, loss of significant customers, etc.
    d. Incorrect. See answer "c".

79. **Solution: d**
    a. Incorrect. This is considered a potential fraud symptom, but so are the other items.
    b. Incorrect. See answer "a".
    c. Incorrect. See answer "a".
    d. Correct. Unsupported transactions, lavish lifestyles, and weak control environments are all considered fraud symptoms that should heighten the auditor's awareness of potential fraud.

80. **Solution: d**
    a. Incorrect. Stratified sampling is a variables sampling procedure. Its primary objective is to estimate a particular population value using the results of a sample. It is not concerned with errors in the population and, therefore, would not stop when the first error is encountered.
    b. Incorrect. Attributes sampling results in an estimate of the rate of occurrence of some characteristic in a population. The sample size is determined to estimate this rate with the desired level of assurance; therefore, the entire sample size is required, regardless of when the first error occurs.
    c. Incorrect. Stop-or-go sampling is a sequential sampling procedure where the next step is determined by the results of the previous step. However, once a step is initiated, it is carried out until it is completed. For example, assume that an internal auditor takes a sample, evaluates the results, and determines additional sample items are required. Each phase of the sample is conducted without reference to when the first error is observed.
    d. Correct. The objective of discovery sampling is to provide a specified level of assurance that a sample will show at least one example of an attribute if the rate of occurrence of that attribute within the population is at or above a specified limit. The audit decision is made once the first error is observed.

81. **Solution: a**
    a. Correct. This is the best procedure because it takes a sample from the total loan file and tests to determine that the loan is properly categorized as well as properly collateralized and aged.
    b. Incorrect. This sample only deals with large dollar items and does not test for proper collateralization.
    c. Incorrect. This is an inefficient audit procedure because it samples from loan applications, not loans approved.
    d. Incorrect. This would be an ineffective procedure because it is based only on loans for which payments are currently being made. It does not include loans that should have been categorized differently because payments are not being made.

82. **Solution: d**
    a. Incorrect. Judgment is needed for confidence levels and sample unit definition.
    b. Incorrect. A statistical sample may result in either a smaller or larger sample.
    c. Incorrect. There is no way to determine which method would produce greater accuracy.
    d. Correct. The only way to have measured reliability (stated in terms of confidence intervals) is to use a statistical sample.

83. **Solution: c**
   a. Incorrect. Attributes sampling is not used for tests of dollar amounts and therefore variability of dollar amounts is not an issue in determining sample size.
   b. Incorrect. Dollar-unit sampling neutralizes variability by defining the sampling unit as an individual dollar.
   c. Correct. Variability affects the standard deviation. The larger the standard deviation, the larger the sample size that is required to achieve a specified level of precision and confidence.
   d. Incorrect. The objective of discovery sampling is to select items until at least one item is selected with a particular characteristic, such as evidence of fraud.

84. **Solution: b**
   a. Incorrect. In the latter instances, there is a definite pattern of increase. This pattern of increase exceeds the upper control limit persistently.
   b. Correct. The model on which the mean, upper, and lower limits are based excludes the persistent exceeding of the upper control limit. Investigation is required.
   c. Incorrect. The upper limit is consistently exceeded. According to the planning model, such occurrences are abnormal.
   d. Incorrect. Portions of the chart appear cyclic, but a significant characteristic is the abnormality exceeding the upper control limit.

85. **Solution: c**
   a. Incorrect. The standard error is not a projection of error in the population.
   b. Incorrect. The standard error is not a measurement of the errors in the sample.
   c. Correct. The standard error is a function of the standard deviation, which is a measurement of the average variation from the mean of the sample. The standard error is used to compute precision and the confidence interval. The larger the standard error, the wider the interval.
   d. Incorrect. The amount of error that the auditor would be willing to accept (the tolerable error) is the auditor's decision; it is not the result of a statistical calculation. The amount of tolerable error has no effect on the standard error.

86. **Solution: c**
   a. Incorrect. This convenience sample is likely to emphasize people with lots of available time at the expense of key employees who are too busy with company work to respond.
   b. Incorrect. Managers and supervisors often do not have the same needs and perceptions as their subordinates and also may misperceive their views.
   c. Correct. Because different employees probably have different situations, needs, and experiences, stratified sampling would best ensure that a representative sample would result.
   d. Incorrect. This approach would produce a disproportionate number of highly paid employees who may not have the same needs as lower-paid employees.

87. **Solution: d**
   a. Incorrect. Answering the questionnaire will help the engagement client identify areas where procedures are weak or not properly documented.
   b. Incorrect. The questionnaire will communicate the areas that the auditor plans to evaluate.
   c. Incorrect. The auditor could use the preparation of the questionnaire to organize the information to be gathered.
   d. Correct. Additional information is useful to the auditor.

88. **Solution: b**
    a. Incorrect. Ratio estimation is a type of variables sampling plan. It is not a technique for estimating standard deviation.
    b. Correct. Auditors use a pilot sample to estimate the standard deviation in a population. This enables the auditor to estimate the confidence interval that would be achieved by the sample, and therefore helps the auditor decide how large of a sample to select.
    c. Incorrect. Auditors use regression to project balances of accounts or other populations.
    d. Incorrect. Discovery sampling is a type of sampling plan, not a technique for estimating standard deviation.

89. **Solution: b**
    a. Incorrect. This is a detailed test, not a study of relationships.
    b. Correct. Analytical tests include comparisons with budgeted amounts, past operations, and similar operations.
    c. Incorrect. This is a detailed test, not a study of relationships.
    d. Incorrect. This is a detailed test, not a study of relationships.

90. **Solution: a**
    a. Correct. If the auditor already suspects fraud, a more directed audit approach would be appropriate.
    b. Incorrect. Relatively stable operating data is a good scenario for using analytical review.
    c. Incorrect. Analytical review would be useful in identifying whether large, non-recurring, or unusual transactions occurred.
    d. Incorrect. Analytical review only needs to have accounts related to other accounts or other independent data. It does not require that they be related to revenue.

91. **Solution: d**
    a. Incorrect. Simple linear regression would be useful, but not as insightful as multiple regression analysis (for example, partition stocks into high volatility and low volatility, as measured by market Beta).
    b. Incorrect. Ratio analysis provides some insight, but it is only designed to provide data on the relative composition of interest-bearing instruments versus stock investments. More information can be gathered through multiple regression.
    c. Incorrect. Trend analysis only verifies that a change has taken place and shows the broad nature of the change. It does not provide insight on the causes of the change in investment income.
    d. Correct. This would be the best approach because it allows the auditor to capture information on the potential causes of the change in investment income.

92. **Solution: b**
    a. Incorrect. Observation will provide evidence on whether the credit personnel are following the procedures while being observed. However, since they know they are being watched, they will probably do what they believe they should do, not what they normally do.
    b. Correct. The purpose of the credit-granting function is to minimize write-offs while at the same time accepting sales likely to result in collection. Reviewing the trend in write-offs will provide some insight concerning the minimization of write-offs.
    c. Incorrect. Responses from the credit manager will lack objectivity, a key attribute of competent evidence.
    d. Incorrect. The credit limits may be set too high or not properly revised periodically. The existence of approval will not detect these problems.

93. **Solution: d**
    a. Incorrect. Because documents are falsified, all supporting documents would match for each cash disbursement.
    b. Incorrect. Vendors would confirm all transactions, because all have been made.
    c. Incorrect. Since fraudulent orders are shipped to another location, the receiving dock procedures would appear correct.
    d. Correct. Because materials are shipped and used in another business, the analytic comparisons would show an unexplained increase in materials used.

94. **Solution: b**
    a. Incorrect. See answer "b".
    b. Correct. The rational decision-making process involves:
        - Recognizing the gap between reality and expectations ("c").
        - Defining the problem (given in the stem).
        - Evaluating the level of acceptable risk associated with a particular decision ("b").
        - Searching for and evaluating solutions to the problem ("a").
        - Choosing a solution.
        - Implementing the solution and measuring results.
    c. Incorrect. See answer "b".
    d. Incorrect. See answer "b".

95. **Solution: a**
    a. Correct. By indicating control weaknesses, flowcharts show where fraud may occur.
    b. Incorrect. Flowcharts do not provide any evidence of the extent of fraud.
    c. Incorrect. Other procedures would be needed to detect where fraud has occurred.
    d. Incorrect. Flowcharts provide evidence of where fraud can occur. Flowcharts therefore help in prevention.

96. **Solution: a**
    a. Correct. Manual forms of recording views and giving group feedback are effective; voting technology can increase the efficiency, but it is not essential to success.
    b. Incorrect. Control self-assessment (CSA) requires facilitation skills.
    c. Incorrect. CSA requires careful planning.
    d. Incorrect. CSA facilitators need to understand and manage group dynamics.

97. **Solution: a (I and II only)**
    I. Correct. If there is no dollar value in the database for existing inventory, this would cause inventory to be understated.
    II. Correct. Inadequate edit checks or uncontrolled borrow/paybacks could cause negative quantities on hand. This would cause inventory to be understated.
    III. Incorrect. If the amount ordered exceeds requirements, this would cause an increase in inventory, but by itself would not cause inventory to be understated or overstated.
    IV. Incorrect. This would have no impact on the valuation of inventory.

98. **Solution: b**
    a. Incorrect. Generalized audit software could be used to search for unusual transactions, such as those exceeding a specific dollar amount.
    b. Correct. It is highly unlikely that the accounts payable system would contain sufficient evidence of fraudulent transactions. Generalized audit software could be used to explore red flags but it would not particularly identify them.
    c. Incorrect. Transaction data could be filtered using generalized audit software.
    d. Incorrect. Suppliers used by cardholders could be summarized using generalized audit software.

99. Solution: d
   a. Incorrect. A more direct test would be needed to accomplish this.
   b. Incorrect. International auditing standards do not require the use of flowcharts.
   c. Incorrect. A more direct test would be needed to accomplish this.
   d. Correct. This is why flowcharting keyed to a narrative is employed by auditors.

100. Solution: b
   a. Incorrect. A vertical flowchart is usually designed to provide for written descriptions.
   b. Correct. By emphasizing the flow of processing between departments and/or people, it more clearly shows any inappropriate separation of duties and lack of independent checks on performance.
   c. Incorrect. It is usually shorter because space for written descriptions is not usually provided.
   d. Incorrect. It follows a transaction from its inception to filing, regardless of departmental lines.

END OF PART II SOLUTIONS

Certified Internal Auditor (CIA) Model Exam Questions

Part III - Business Analysis and Information Technology

Part III Model Exam Questions: 100

Questions on actual CIA Exam Part III: 125
(see explanation in "Foreword" on page iii)

Time allowed for completion of CIA Exam Part III: 210 minutes

Instructions such as those that follow will be listed on the cover of each CIA examination. Please read them carefully.

1. Place your candidate number on the answer sheet in the space provided.
2. Do not place extraneous marks on the answer sheet.
3. Be certain that changes to answers are **completely** erased.
4. All references to the *Professional Practices Framework* refer to The IIA's *Professional Practices Framework*, which includes the *Standards* and the *Practice Advisories*. All references to *Standards* refer to the *International Standards for the Professional Practice of Internal Auditing* outlined in The IIA's *Professional Practices Framework*.

Failure to follow these instructions and the "Instructions to Candidates" guidelines could adversely affect both your right to receive the results of this examination and your future participation in the Certified Internal Auditor program.

All papers submitted in completion of any part of this examination become the sole property of The Institute of Internal Auditors, Inc. Candidates may not disclose the contents of this exam unless expressly authorized by the Certification Department.

1. The costs of quality that are incurred in detecting units of product that do not conform to product specifications are referred to as:
   a. Prevention costs.
   b. Appraisal costs.
   c. Rework costs.
   d. Failure costs.

2. The use of teams in total quality management is important because:
   a. Well-managed teams can be highly creative and are able to address complex problems better than individuals can.
   b. Teams are quicker to make decisions, thereby helping to reduce cycle time.
   c. Employee motivation is higher for team members than for individual contributors.
   d. The use of teams eliminates the need for supervision, thereby allowing a company to become leaner and more profitable.

3. Which of the following is a major element of the ISO 9000:2000 quality management system standards?
   a. The principle that improved employee satisfaction will lead to increased productivity.
   b. The attitude and actions of the board and management regarding the significance of control within the organization.
   c. The assessment of the risk that objectives are not achieved.
   d. A requirement for organizations to monitor information on customer satisfaction as a measure of performance.

4. The sales manager for a builder of custom yachts developed the following conditional table for annual production and sales:

Demand	10	20	30	50
Probability	0.1	0.2	0.5	0.2

Yachts Built	Expected Profit			
10	10	10	10	10
20	0	20	20	20
30	-10	10	30	30
50	-30	-10	10	50

   According to the table, how many yachts should be built?
   a. 10.
   b. 20.
   c. 30.
   d. 50.

5. All of the following are useful for forecasting the needed level of inventory **except**:
   a. Knowledge of the behavior of business cycles.
   b. Internal accounting allocations of costs to different segments of the company.
   c. Information about seasonal variations in demand.
   d. Econometric modeling.

6. The process of adding resources to shorten selected activity times on the critical path in project scheduling is called:
   a. Crashing.
   b. The Delphi technique.
   c. ABC analysis.
   d. A branch-and-bound solution.

7. The following information applies to a project:

Activity	Time (days)	Immediate Predecessor
A	5	None
B	3	None
C	4	A
D	2	B
E	6	C, D

   The earliest completion time for the project is:
   a. 11 days.
   b. 14 days.
   c. 15 days.
   d. 20 days.

8. Which of the following will allow a manufacturer with limited resources to maximize profits?
   a. The Delphi technique.
   b. Exponential smoothing.
   c. Regression analysis.
   d. Linear programming.

9. A means of limiting production delays caused by equipment breakdown and repair is to:
   a. Schedule production based on capacity planning.
   b. Plan maintenance activity based on an analysis of equipment repair work orders.
   c. Pre-authorize equipment maintenance and overtime pay.
   d. Establish a preventive maintenance program for all production equipment.

10. To remove the effect of seasonal variation from a time series, original data should be:
    a. Increased by the seasonal factor.
    b. Reduced by the seasonal factor.
    c. Multiplied by the seasonal factor.
    d. Divided by the seasonal factor.

11. An advantage of using bar codes rather than other means of identification of parts used by a manufacturer is that:
    a. The movement of all parts is controlled.
    b. The movement of parts is easily and quickly recorded.
    c. Vendors can use the same part numbers.
    d. Vendors use the same identification methods.

12. An appropriate technique for planning and controlling manufacturing inventories, such as raw materials, components, and sub-assemblies, whose demand depends on the level of production is:
    a. Materials requirements planning.
    b. Regression analysis.
    c. Capital budgeting.
    d. Linear programming.

13. If a just-in-time purchasing policy is successful in reducing the total inventory costs of a manufacturing company, which of the following combinations of cost changes would be most likely to occur?
    a. An increase in purchasing costs and a decrease in stockout costs.
    b. An increase in purchasing costs and a decrease in quality costs.
    c. An increase in quality costs and a decrease in ordering costs.
    d. An increase in stockout costs and a decrease in carrying costs.

14. In an economic order quantity (EOQ) model, both the costs per order and the holding costs are estimates. If those estimates are varied to determine how much the changes affect the optimal EOQ, such analysis would be called a:
    a. Forecasting model.
    b. Sensitivity analysis.
    c. Critical path method analysis.
    d. Decision analysis.

15. When film is sold for use with a camera, this is an example of which of the following product mix pricing strategies?
    a. By-product pricing.
    b. Optional product pricing.
    c. Captive product pricing.
    d. Product bundle pricing.

16. A competitive marketing strategy in which a firm specializes in serving customers overlooked or ignored by major competitors is called a:
    a. Market leader strategy.
    b. Market challenger strategy.
    c. Market follower strategy.
    d. Market niche strategy.

17. Which of the following hiring procedures provides the most control over the accuracy of information submitted on an employment application?
    a. Applicants are required to submit unofficial copies of their transcripts along with the application as verification of their educational credentials.
    b. The hiring organization calls the last place of employment for each finalist to verify the employment length and position held.
    c. Letters of recommendation which attest to the applicant's character must be mailed directly to the hiring organization rather than being submitted by the applicant.
    d. Applicants are required to sign that the information on the applicant is true and correct as a confirmation of the truth of the information in the application.

18. A balanced scorecard is primarily concerned with:
    a. Staff.
    b. Structure.
    c. Strategy.
    d. Systems.

19. The practice of recording advanced payments from customers as liabilities is an application of the:
    a. Going concern assumption.
    b. Monetary unit assumption.
    c. Historic cost principle.
    d. Revenue recognition principle.

20. Which of the following is an example of a contingent liability?
    a. A retail store in a shopping mall pays the lessor a minimum monthly rent plus an agreed-upon percentage of sales.
    b. A company is refusing to pay the invoice for the annual audit because it seems higher than the amount agreed upon with the public accounting firm's partner.
    c. A company accrues income tax payable in its interim financial statements.
    d. A lessee agrees to reimburse a lessor for a shortfall in the residual value of an asset under lease.

21. Which must be part of any risk model involving inventory valuation?
    a. Product warranty policies.
    b. Vendor pricing policies.
    c. Inventory shrinkage expense.
    d. Annual sales forecasts.

22. A company uses straight-line depreciation for financial reporting purposes, but uses accelerated depreciation for tax purposes. Which of the following account balances would be lower in the financial statements used for tax purposes than it would be in the general purpose financial statements?
    a. Accumulated depreciation.
    b. Cash.
    c. Retained earnings.
    d. Gross fixed assets.

23. Under a defined contribution pension plan, <List A> is reported on the balance sheet only if the amount the organization has contributed to the pension trust is <List B> the amount required.

	List A	List B
a.	An asset	Greater than
b.	An asset	Equal to
c.	A liability	Greater than
d.	A liability	Equal to

24. If a lease agreement transfers substantially all of the benefits and risks of ownership of the asset to the lessee, the asset value is recognized on the lessee's books as <List A> asset and the lease is <List B> lease.

	List A	List B
a.	A tangible	A capital
b.	An intangible	A capital
c.	A tangible	An operating
d.	An intangible	An operating

25. Which of the following securities is likely to have the **least** risk?
    a. Income bonds.
    b. Debentures.
    c. Subordinated debentures.
    d. First-mortgage bonds.

26. A U.S. company and a European company purchased the same stock on a European stock exchange and held the stock for one year. If the value of the euro weakened against the U.S. dollar during the period, in comparison with the European company's return, the U.S. company's return will be:
    a. Lower.
    b. Higher.
    c. The same.
    d. Indeterminate from the information provided.

27. In a two-tier merger offer, shareholders receive a higher amount per share if they:
    a. Agree to purchase newly issued bonds in the combined firm.
    b. Agree to sell back to the firm any bonds that they currently own.
    c. Tender their stock later.
    d. Tender their stock earlier.

28. Which combination of ratios can be used to derive return on equity?
    a. Market value to book value ratio and total debt to total assets ratio.
    b. Price to earnings ratio, earnings per share, and net profit margin.
    c. Price to earnings ratio and return on assets.
    d. Net profit margin, asset turnover, and equity multiplier.

29. Which of the following is true about the impact of price inflation on financial ratio analysis?
    a. Inflation impacts only those ratios computed from balance sheet accounts.
    b. Inflation impacts financial ratio analysis for one firm over time, but not comparative analysis of firms of different ages.
    c. Inflation impacts financial ratio analysis for one firm over time, as well as comparative analysis of firms of different ages.
    d. Inflation impacts comparative analysis of firms of different ages, but not financial ratio analysis for one firm over time.

30. The difference between the required rate of return on a given risky investment and that of a risk-free investment with the same expected return is the:
    a. Risk premium.
    b. Coefficient of variation.
    c. Standard error of measurement.
    d. Beta coefficient.

31. Capital structure decisions involve determining the proportions of financing from:
    a. Short-term or long-term debt.
    b. Debt or equity.
    c. Short-term or long-term assets.
    d. Retained earnings or common stock.

32. If bonds are sold at a discount and the effective interest method of amortization is used, interest expense will:
    a. Increase from one period to another.
    b. Remain constant from one period to another.
    c. Equal the cash interest payment each period.
    d. Be less than the cash interest payment each period.

33. If a high percentage of a firm's total costs is fixed, the firm's operating leverage will be:
    a. High.
    b. Low.
    c. Unchanged.
    d. Unable to be determined.

34. When comparing two companies, if all else is equal, the company that has a higher dividend payout ratio will have a:
    a. Higher marginal cost of capital.
    b. Lower debt ratio.
    c. Higher investment opportunity schedule.
    d. Higher price to earnings ratio.

35. Why would a company maintain a compensating cash balance?
    a. To make routine payments and collections.
    b. To pay for banking services.
    c. To provide a reserve in case of unforeseen fluctuations in cash flows.
    d. To take advantage of bargain purchase opportunities that may arise.

36. The efficient markets theory implies that securities prices are:
    a. Not a good estimate of future cash flows.
    b. Fair and a reflection of all publicly available information.
    c. Not the best benchmark for corporate financial decisions.
    d. Always less than their fair value.

Use the following graph to answer questions 37 through 38.

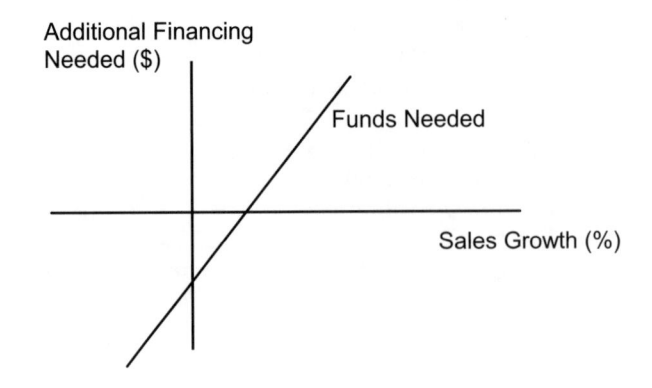

37. If all else is equal, firms with higher profit margins require less additional financing for any sales growth rate. If the profit margin of a company increased, the funds-needed line would shift:
    a. Up and become less steep.
    b. Up and become more steep.
    c. Down and become less steep.
    d. Down and become more steep.

38. The funds-needed line does not pass through the origin unless the firm has a:
    a. 100 percent dividend payout policy.
    b. Zero percent dividend payout policy.
    c. 100 percent sales growth rate.
    d. Zero percent sales growth rate.

Use the following information to answer questions 39 through 40.

On January 1, a company has no opening inventory balance. The following purchases are made during the year:

	Units Purchased	Unit Cost
January 1	5,000	$10.00
April 1	5,000	$9.00
July 1	5,000	$8.00
October 1	5,000	$7.50

There are 10,000 units in inventory on December 31.

39. If the company uses the first-in, first-out (FIFO) method of inventory valuation, the ending inventory balance will be:
    a. $77,500.
    b. $85,000.
    c. $86,250.
    d. $95,000.

40. If the company uses the last-in, first-out (LIFO) method of inventory valuation, cost of goods sold for the year will be:
    a. $77,500.
    b. $86,250.
    c. $87,500.
    d. $95,000.

41. The economic value of a firm will rise following an increase in:
    a. Net cash flow.
    b. Systematic risk.
    c. Unsystematic risk.
    d. The discount rate.

42. Abnormal spoilage is:
    a. Not expected to occur when standard costs are used.
    b. Not usually controllable by the production supervisor.
    c. The result of unrealistic production standards.
    d. Not expected to occur under efficient operating conditions.

43. Which of the following is a product cost for a manufacturing company?
    a. Insurance on the corporate headquarters building.
    b. Property taxes on a factory.
    c. Depreciation on a salesperson's vehicle.
    d. The salary of a sales manager.

Use the following information to answer questions 44 through 45.

A firm with an 18 percent cost of capital is considering the following projects (on January 1 of year one):

	Jan. 1, Year One, Cash Outflow (000's Omitted)	Dec. 31, Year Five, Cash Inflow (000's Omitted)	Project Internal Rate of Return
Project A	$3,500	$7,400	15%
Project B	$4,000	$9,950	?

Present Value of $1 Due at the End of "N" Periods

N	12%	14%	15%	16%	18%	20%	22%
4	.6355	.5921	.5718	.5523	.5158	.4823	.4230
5	.5674	.5194	.4972	.4761	.4371	.4019	.3411
6	.5066	.4556	.4323	.4104	.3704	.3349	.2751

44. Using the net present value method, project A's net present value is:
    a. $(316,920).
    b. $(265,460).
    c. $0.
    d. $316,920.

45. Project B's internal rate of return is closest to:
    a. 15 percent.
    b. 18 percent.
    c. 20 percent.
    d. 22 percent.

46. A flexible budget is a quantitative expression of a plan that:
    a. Is developed for the actual level of output achieved for the budget period.
    b. Is comprised of the budgeted income statement and its supporting schedules for a budget period.
    c. Focuses on the costs of activities necessary to produce and sell products and services for a budget period.
    d. Projects costs on the basis of future improvements in existing practices and procedures during a budget period.

47. A domestic company has sales divisions in country X and country Y. The company sells only one product, which costs $20 per unit to produce. There are no trade barriers or tariffs among the three countries. Information specific to each of the three countries is as follows:

Country	Corporate Tax Rate	Before-Tax Selling Price	Quantity Sold	Additional Costs
Home	50%	$30	1,500	$10,000
X	60%	$40	1,000	$12,500
Y	40%	$35	2,000	$11,000

When selling items to its sales division(s) in <List A>, the company should set the <List B> allowable transfer price.

    List A   List B
a. Countries X and Y   Highest
b. Countries X and Y   Lowest
c. Country X   Highest
d. Country Y   Highest

48. A master budget:
    a. Shows forecasted and actual results.
    b. Contains only controllable costs.
    c. Can be used to determine manufacturing cost variances.
    d. Contains the operating budget.

49. A company produced and sold 100,000 units of a component with a variable cost of $20 per unit. Of the units produced, 1,200 failed the company's tolerance specifications and were reworked at a cost of $12 per unit. Reworked units were sold as factory seconds at $45 each, and first-quality units were sold at $50 each. If the company had implemented a quality assurance program to ensure that all units produced conformed to specifications, the increase in the company's contribution margin from this component would have been:
    a. $14,400.
    b. $20,400.
    c. $21,600.
    d. $39,600.

50. A company has excess capacity in production-related fixed assets. If in a given year these fixed assets were being used to only 80 percent of capacity and the sales level in that year was $2,000,000, the full capacity sales level is:
    a. $1,600,000.
    b. $2,000,000.
    c. $2,500,000.
    d. $10,000,000.

Use the following information to answer questions 51 through 52.

A company harvests, packs, and ships all of its own produce. The company operates three packing lines. A summary of completed inventory costs is as follows:

Packing-line employee salary expense	$150,000
Packing-line supervision salary expense	$90,000
Quality control salary expense	$30,000
Packing crates expense	$15,000
Electricity expense	$3,000
Depreciation expense	$66,000

51. Costs for the packing lines would be accumulated in part by:
    a. Recording payroll expense by employee job category.
    b. Computing depreciation expense.
    c. Producing monthly financial statements.
    d. Forecasting monthly material shortages.

52. At the end of the reporting period, 600,000 units had been packed and shipped. No inventory remained on hand. If the company used process costing, the cost per unit would be:
    a. $0.197
    b. $0.275
    c. $0.315
    d. $0.590

53. Which of the following would be a reasonable basis for allocating the material handling costs to the units produced in an activity-based costing system?
    a. Number of production runs per year.
    b. Number of components per completed unit.
    c. Amount of time required to produce one unit.
    d. Amount of overhead applied to each completed unit.

54. Residual income is often preferred over return on investment (ROI) as a performance evaluation because:
    a. Residual income is a measure over time while ROI represents the results for a single time period.
    b. Residual income concentrates on maximizing absolute dollars of income rather than a percentage return as with ROI.
    c. The imputed interest rate used in calculating residual income is more easily derived than the target rate that is compared to the calculated ROI.
    d. Average investment is employed with residual income while year-end investment is employed with ROI.

55. Which of the following costs are **not** relevant in a special-order decision?
    a. Incremental costs.
    b. Opportunity costs.
    c. Outlay costs.
    d. Sunk costs.

56. Which of the following is a tool of monetary policy that a nation's central bank could use to stabilize the economy during an inflationary period?
    a. Selling government securities.
    b. Lowering bank reserve requirements.
    c. Lowering bank discount rates.
    d. Encouraging higher tax rates.

57. If a country uses trade quotas to overcome chronic trade deficits, the most likely outcome would be that:
    a. Unemployment and productivity rates will rise.
    b. Unemployment rates will rise and productivity rates will decline.
    c. Unemployment rates will decline and productivity rates will rise.
    d. Unemployment and productivity rates will decline.

58. Which of the following correctly describes the introduction of a government tax credit on investments?
    a. Corporate investments will have higher net present values, all else equal, than without the tax credit.
    b. Tax credits on investments are designed to restrain inflation.
    c. Tax credits on investments increase investment costs, and all else equal, reduce the level of corporate investment.
    d. Tax credits on investments are taxes that are typically levied on individual projects rather than on groups of projects.

59. Revenue tariffs are designed to:
    a. Develop new export opportunities.
    b. Provide the government with tax revenues.
    c. Restrict the amount of a commodity that can be imported in a given period.
    d. Encourage foreign companies to limit the amount of their exports to a particular country.

60. A company would like to contract for janitorial services for one year with four option years. The specifications require the potential contractor to perform certain cleaning services at specified intervals. Which of the following is the best contract type for this requirement?
    a. Cost-reimbursable.
    b. Indefinite delivery.
    c. Fixed-price.
    d. Time-and-materials.

61. Which of the following refers to taxes that do **not** necessarily take a larger absolute share of an increase in income?
    a. Progressive.
    b. Proportional.
    c. Regressive.
    d. Flat.

62. Temporary and permanent differences between taxable income and pre-tax financial income differ in that:
    a. Temporary differences do not give rise to future taxable or deductible amounts.
    b. Only permanent differences have deferred tax consequences.
    c. Only temporary differences have deferred tax consequences.
    d. Temporary differences include items that enter into pre-tax financial income but never into taxable income.

63. A value-added tax is collected on the basis of:
    a. The difference between the value of a company's sales and the value of its purchases from other domestic companies.
    b. The difference between the selling price of real property and the price the company originally paid for the property.
    c. The value of a company's sales to related companies.
    d. The profit earned on a company's sales.

64. The gross national product will fall following an increase in:
    a. Consumption expenditures.
    b. Imports.
    c. Exports.
    d. Inflation.

65. Which of the following is **not** a typical output control?
    a. Reviewing the computer processing logs to determine that all of the correct computer jobs executed properly.
    b. Matching input data with information on master files and placing unmatched items in a suspense file.
    c. Periodically reconciling output reports to make sure that totals, formats, and critical details are correct and agree with input.
    d. Maintaining formal procedures and documentation specifying authorized recipients of output reports, checks, or other critical documents.

66. Minimizing the likelihood of unauthorized editing of production programs, job control language, and operating system software can best be accomplished by:
    a. Database access reviews.
    b. Compliance reviews.
    c. Good change control procedures.
    d. Effective network security software.

67. Which control, when implemented, would best assist in meeting the control objective that a system have the capability to hold users accountable for functions performed?
    a. Programmed cutoff.
    b. Redundant hardware.
    c. Activity logging.
    d. Transaction error logging.

68. Image processing systems have the potential to reduce the volume of paper circulated throughout an organization. To reduce the likelihood of users relying on the wrong images, management should ensure that appropriate controls exist to maintain the:
    a. Legibility of image data.
    b. Accessibility of image data.
    c. Integrity of index data.
    d. Initial sequence of index data.

69. Both users and management approve the initial proposal, design specifications, conversion plan, and testing plan of an information system. This is an example of:
    a. Implementation controls.
    b. Hardware controls.
    c. Computer operations controls.
    d. Data security controls.

70. A device used to connect dissimilar networks is a:
    a. Gateway.
    b. Bridge.
    c. Router.
    d. Wiring concentrator.

71. A total interruption of processing throughout a distributed information technology system can be minimized through the use of:
    a. Exception reporting.
    b. Fail-soft protection.
    c. Backup and recovery.
    d. Data file security.

72. To avoid invalid data input, a bank added an extra number at the end of each account number and subjected the new number to an algorithm. This technique is known as:
    a. Optical character recognition.
    b. A check digit.
    c. A dependency check.
    d. A format check.

73. Successful electronic data interchange (EDI) implementation begins with which of the following?
    a. Mapping the work processes and flows that support the organization's goals.
    b. Purchasing new hardware for the EDI system.
    c. Selecting reliable vendors for translation and communication software.
    d. Standardizing transaction formats and data.

74. A company using electronic data interchange (EDI) made it a practice to track the functional acknowledgments from trading partners and to issue warning messages if acknowledgments did not occur within a reasonable length of time. What risk was the company attempting to address by this practice?
    a. Transactions that have not originated from a legitimate trading partner may be inserted into the EDI network.
    b. Transmission of EDI transactions to trading partners may sometimes fail.
    c. There may be disagreement between the parties as to whether the EDI transactions form a legal contract.
    d. EDI data may not be accurately and completely processed by the EDI software.

75. What technique could be used to prevent the input of alphabetic characters into an all numeric identification number?
    a. An existence check.
    b. A check digit.
    c. A dependency check.
    d. A format check.

76. A manufacturer of complex electronic equipment such as oscilloscopes and microscopes has been shipping its products with thick paper manuals but wants to reduce the cost of producing and shipping this documentation. Of the following, the best medium for the manufacturer to use to accomplish this is:
    a. Write-once-read-many.
    b. Digital audio tape.
    c. Compact disc/read-only memory.
    d. Computer-output-to-microform.

77. In a large organization, the biggest risk in **not** having an adequately staffed information center help desk is:
    a. Increased difficulty in performing application audits.
    b. Inadequate documentation for application systems.
    c. Increased likelihood of use of unauthorized program code.
    d. Persistent errors in user interaction with systems.

78. What technology is needed in order to convert a paper document into a computer file?
    a. Optical character recognition.
    b. Electronic data interchange.
    c. Bar-code scanning.
    d. Joining and merging.

79. Utility programs can be used to read files which contain all authorized access user codes for a server. A control to prevent this is:
    a. Internally encrypted passwords.
    b. A password hierarchy.
    c. Log-on passwords.
    d. A peer-to-peer network.

80. Which of the following is a malicious program, the purpose of which is to reproduce itself throughout the network and produce a denial of service attack by excessively utilizing system resources?
    a. Logic bomb.
    b. Virus.
    c. Worm.
    d. Trojan horse.

81. Unauthorized alteration of on-line records can be prevented by employing:
    a. Key verification.
    b. Computer sequence checks.
    c. Computer matching.
    d. Database access controls.

82. Which of the following statements are correct regarding electronic mail security?

    I. Electronic mail can be no more secure than the computer system on which it operates.
    II. Confidential electronic mail messages should be stored on the mail server as electronic mail for the same length of time as similar paper-based documents.
    III. In larger organizations, there may be several electronic mail administrators and locations with varying levels of security.

    a. I only.
    b. I and II only.
    c. I and III only.
    d. II and III only.

83. Which of the following would provide the **least** security for sensitive data stored on a notebook computer?
    a. Encrypting data files on the notebook computer.
    b. Using password protection for the screen-saver program on the notebook computer.
    c. Using a notebook computer with a removable hard disk drive.
    d. Locking the notebook computer in a case when not in use.

84. Which of the following would be of greatest concern to an auditor reviewing a policy regarding the sale of a company's used personal computers to outside parties?
    a. Whether deleted files on the hard disk drive have been completely erased.
    b. Whether the computer has viruses.
    c. Whether all software on the computer is properly licensed.
    d. Whether there is terminal emulation software on the computer.

85. Which of the following would **not** be appropriate to consider in the physical design of a data center?
    a. Evaluation of potential risks from railroad lines and highways.
    b. Use of biometric access systems.
    c. Design of authorization tables for operating system access.
    d. Inclusion of an uninterruptible power supply system and surge protection.

86. Inefficient usage of excess computer equipment can be controlled by:
    a. Contingency planning.
    b. System feasibility studies.
    c. Capacity planning.
    d. Exception reporting.

87. An electronics company has decided to implement a new system through the use of rapid application development techniques. Which of the following would be included in the development of the new system?
    a. Deferring the need for system documentation until the final modules are completed.
    b. Removing project management responsibilities from the development teams.
    c. Creating the system module by module until completed.
    d. Using object development techniques to minimize the use of previous code.

88. A bank is developing a computer system to help evaluate loan applications. The information systems (IS) staff interview the bank's mortgage underwriters to extract their knowledge and decision processes for input into the computer system. The completed system should be able to process information the same as do the underwriters and make final recommendations regarding loan decisions. This approach is called:
    a. An expert system.
    b. A neural network.
    c. An intelligent agent.
    d. Fuzzy logic.

89. User acceptance testing is more important in an object-oriented development process than in a traditional environment because of the implications of the:
    a. Absence of design documentation.
    b. Lack of a tracking system for changes.
    c. Potential for continuous monitoring.
    d. Inheritance of properties in hierarchies.

90. The best evidence that contingency planning is effective is to have:
    a. No processing interruptions during the past year.
    b. Comprehensive documentation of the plan.
    c. Signoff on the plan by the internal audit activity.
    d. Successful testing of the plan.

91. Which of the following actions would best address a concern that data uploaded from a desktop computer may be erroneous?
    a. The mainframe computer should be backed up on a regular basis.
    b. Two persons should be present at the desktop computer when it is uploading data.
    c. The mainframe computer should subject the data to the same edits and validation routines that on-line data entry would require.
    d. Users should be required to review a random sample of processed data.

92. A password is an example of:
    a. A physical control.
    b. An edit control.
    c. A digital control.
    d. An access control.

93. Preventing someone with sufficient technical skill from circumventing security procedures and making changes to production programs is best accomplished by:
    a. Reviewing reports of jobs completed.
    b. Comparing production programs with independently controlled copies.
    c. Running test data periodically.
    d. Providing suitable segregation of duties.

94. To reduce security exposure when transmitting proprietary data over communication lines, a company should use:
    a. Asynchronous modems.
    b. Authentication techniques.
    c. Call-back procedures.
    d. Cryptographic devices.

95. Which of the following security controls would best prevent unauthorized access to sensitive data through an unattended data terminal directly connected to a mainframe?
    a. Use of a screen-saver with a password.
    b. Use of workstation scripts.
    c. Encryption of data files.
    d. Automatic log-off of inactive users.

96. Which of the following access setups is appropriate in a computer environment?

	Update Access for Production Data		Update Access for Production Programs	
	Users Have?	Application Programmers Have?	Users Have?	Application Programmers Have?
a.	Yes	No	No	No
b.	Yes	No	No	Yes
c.	No	Yes	Yes	No
d.	No	Yes	Yes	Yes

97. Computer program libraries can best be kept secure by:
    a. Installing a logging system for program access.
    b. Monitoring physical access to program library media.
    c. Restricting physical and logical access.
    d. Denying access from remote terminals.

98. What language interface would a database administrator use to establish the structure of database tables?
    a. Data definition language.
    b. Data control language.
    c. Data manipulation language.
    d. Data query language.

99. Query facilities for a database system would most likely include all of the following **except**:
    a. Graphical output capability.
    b. Data dictionary access.
    c. A data validity checker.
    d. A query-by-example interface.

100. The most difficult aspect of using Internet resources is:
    a. Making a physical connection.
    b. Locating the best information source.
    c. Obtaining the equipment required.
    d. Getting authorization for access.

END OF PART III QUESTIONS

PLEASE NOTE: The actual CIA exam Part III will contain *125 exam questions*. The 125 questions will include up to 25 unscored questions, which will be used for research purposes. These unscored questions will be interspersed with the scored questions and will not be identified as unscored questions. Candidates should therefore answer all 125 questions to the best of their ability.

Solutions for Part III – Business Analysis and Information Technology

The solutions and suggested explanations for Part III of the Certified Internal Auditor Model Exam Questions are provided on the following pages.

The chart below cross-references the question numbers for Part III with the topics tested:

Topic Tested	Question Number
Business Processes	1 – 18
Financial Accounting and Finance	19 – 41
Managerial Accounting	42 – 55
Regulatory, Legal, and Economics	56 – 64
Information Technology	65 – 100

1. **Solution: b**
   a. Incorrect. Prevention costs are incurred to prevent the production of products that do not conform to specifications.
   b. Correct. Appraisal costs are those costs (such as test equipment maintenance and destructive testing) incurred to detect which products do not conform to specifications.
   c. Incorrect. Rework costs, a type of failure cost, are incurred when a nonconforming product is detected and corrections are made.
   d. Incorrect. Failure costs are incurred in the repair of nonconforming products.

2. **Solution: a**
   a. Correct. Teams can use the diverse knowledge and skills of all team members.
   b. Incorrect. Teams are often inefficient and costly.
   c. Incorrect. Although employee motivation may be high in teams, the high motivation does not always translate directly to quality improvement.
   d. Incorrect. Although need for supervision may be reduced, it is not eliminated.

3. **Solution: d**
   a. Incorrect. This is not a part of the ISO 9000 standards. ISO argues that following the eight management principles that underlie the ISO 9000 standards will lead to improved employee satisfaction.
   b. Incorrect. This is the control environment as defined in the glossary of The IIA's Standards; there is no direct reference to any such concept in the ISO 9000 standards.
   c. Incorrect. The ISO 9000 approach does not take a risk assessment approach; a risk assessment approach is what underlies internal auditing.
   d. Correct. This is one of the major changes to the ISO 9000 standards made in the 2000 revision.

4. **Solution: c**
   To achieve the maximum expected profit, 30 yachts should be built. For each level of production, multiply the probability of demand by the expected profit:
   a. Incorrect. Computation: 0.1($10)+0.2($10)+0.5($10)+0.2($10) = $10.
   b. Incorrect. Computation: 0.1($0)+0.2($20)+0.5($20)+0.2($20) = $18.
   c. Correct. Computation: 0.1(-$10)+0.2($10)+0.5($30)+0.2($30) = $22.
   d. Incorrect. Computation: 0.1(-$30)+0.2(-$10)+0.5($10)+0.2($50) = $10.

5. **Solution: b**
   a. Incorrect. Knowing the behavior of business cycles, understanding seasonal variations in demand for the product, and using econometric models can be valuable when forecasting the required purchases of inventory.
   b. Correct. Internal accounting allocations of costs to different segments of the company are arbitrary assignments of already incurred costs that do not have anything to do with forecasting demand.
   c. Incorrect. See answer "a".
   d. Incorrect. See answer "a".

6. **Solution: a**
   a. Correct. Crashing is the process of adding resources to shorten activity times on the critical path in project scheduling.
   b. Incorrect. The Delphi technique is a qualitative forecasting approach.
   c. Incorrect. ABC analysis is an inventory model.
   d. Incorrect. The branch-and-bound solution is an integer programming solution.

7. **Solution: c**
   a. Incorrect. Eleven days is the shortest, not the longest, time to completion.
   b. Incorrect. Fourteen days sums 5 + 3 + 6, but is not a path to completion.
   c. Correct. The two paths are 5 + 4 + 6 = 15 days, and 3 + 2 + 6 = 11 days. The longest path, and therefore the earliest completion time, is 15 days.
   d. Incorrect. Twenty days is the sum of all of the activity times.

8. **Solution: d**
   a. Incorrect. The Delphi technique is a qualitative forecasting method that obtains forecasts through group consensus.
   b. Incorrect. Exponential smoothing is a forecasting technique that uses past time series values to arrive at forecasted values.
   c. Incorrect. Regression analysis is a statistical technique used to develop forecasts based on the relationship between two or more variables.
   d. Correct. Linear programming is a mathematical technique for maximizing or minimizing a given objective subject to certain constraints. It is the correct technique to optimize the problem of limited resources.

9. **Solution: d**
   a. Incorrect. Scheduling production based on capacity utilization ignores other important factors such as demands.
   b. Incorrect. Budgeting maintenance department activities based on previous work orders will not prevent equipment breakdowns and repairs.
   c. Incorrect. Standing authorizations of work orders and overtime will not address the problem posed.
   d. Correct. A preventive maintenance program will reduce equipment breakdowns and repairs.

10. **Solution: d**
    a. Incorrect. See answer "d".
    b. Incorrect. See answer "d".
    c. Incorrect. See answer "d".
    d. Correct. If the original data (with the four trends) is divided by the seasonal norm, the seasonal component is factored out of the data.

11. **Solution: b**
    a. Incorrect. The movement of parts can escape being recorded with any identification method.
    b. Correct. A reason to use bar codes rather than other means of identification is to record the movement of parts with minimal labor costs.
    c. Incorrect. Each vendor has its own part-numbering scheme, which is unlikely to correspond to the buyer's scheme.
    d. Incorrect. Each vendor has its own identification method, although vendors in the same industry often cooperate to minimize the number of bar-code systems that they use.

12. **Solution: a**
    a. Correct. Materials requirements planning (MRP) is a planning and controlling technique for managing dependent-demand manufacturing inventories.
    b. Incorrect. Regression analysis is a statistical procedure for estimating the relation between variables.
    c. Incorrect. Capital budgeting is used for analyzing and evaluating long-term capital investments.
    d. Incorrect. Linear programming is a mathematical technique for maximizing or minimizing a given objective subject to certain constraints.

13. **Solution: d**
    a. Incorrect. The supplier may ask for a concession in its selling price, which would raise the manufacturer's purchasing costs. However, the manufacturing company will be receiving fewer materials at any point in time, increasing the likelihood of stockout and thereby resulting in an increase in stockout costs.
    b. Incorrect. The supplier may ask for a concession in its selling price, which would raise the manufacturer's purchasing costs. However, the cost of quality would not necessarily be affected by the just-in-time purchasing system.
    c. Incorrect. With fewer purchase orders being processed by the manufacturer, the ordering costs are likely to decrease. However, the cost of quality would not necessarily be affected by the just-in-time purchasing system.
    d. Correct. In this situation, the company will be receiving fewer materials at any point in time, increasing the likelihood of stockout and thereby resulting in an increase in stockout costs. At the same time, the average inventory will be less, resulting in a reduction in the carrying costs.

14. **Solution: b**
    a. Incorrect. Forecasting models involve projecting data over time or developing regression models when time series data are not available.
    b. Correct. An economic order quantity (EOQ) sensitivity analysis involves varying the holding costs per unit and/or the order costs to determine how much the changes affect the optimal EOQ.
    c. Incorrect. Critical path method involves project scheduling.
    d. Incorrect. Decision analysis involves selecting the best option from alternatives.

15. **Solution: c**
    a. Incorrect. There are no additional costs incurred other than storage and delivery for the development of this product. Therefore, the manufacturer will make a profit on any price over the cost of storage and delivery.
    b. Incorrect. Optional products are those offered for sale along with the main product. They are unlikely to have zero production cost so the seller must receive a price above the storage and delivery costs for such products.
    c. Correct. Captive products are those that must be used along with the main product. Sellers often make their money on the captive products, rather than on the main product that is sold at a low price. The captive products therefore will be priced well above the storage and delivery costs.
    d. Incorrect. Product bundles are combinations of products sold together at a reduced price, such as season tickets for a theater. Products are bundled in order to promote the sale of certain items that consumers might not otherwise purchase. The combined price of the bundle must be low enough to encourage consumers to buy the bundle, but must recover production costs and provide some profit for the seller. The price must exceed storage and delivery costs.

16. **Solution: d**
    a. Incorrect. Market leader strategies are employed by the major competitors that dominate a market
    b. Incorrect. Market challenger strategies are followed by runner-up companies that aggressively attack competitors to get more market share.
    c. Incorrect. Market follower strategies are used by runner-up companies that follow competitor's product offers, pricing, and market programs.
    d. Correct. Specializing in serving customers overlooked or ignored by major competitors is a market niche strategy. This strategy specializes along market, customer, product, or marketing mix lines.

17. **Solution: b**
    a. Incorrect. The applicant is providing the transcript, leading to a loss of independence. In addition, the transcript is unofficial, making it very easy to change the information and send a photocopy of the altered transcript.
    b. Correct. This represents an independent verification of employment since the hiring organization is performing the verification process.
    c. Incorrect. There is nothing to prevent the applicants from writing the letters themselves, putting fraudulent return address information on the letters, and mailing them.
    d. Incorrect. If an applicant is going to lie about information, there is no reason to believe that the applicant will not sign the applicant's own name to the fraudulent information. This is not an independent verification.

18. **Solution: c**
    a. Incorrect. Although a balanced scorecard should be developed with staff in mind, the primary aim is the alignment of performance measures with strategy.
    b. Incorrect. Structure should be created after the scorecard has been developed to ensure that responsibilities, competencies and measures are appropriate to achieve the agreed-upon strategies.
    c. Correct. The scorecard is primarily a tool to assist the organization in describing and clarifying its strategy and then alignment of its performance measures to that strategy.
    d. Incorrect. Systems are a means to achieving objectives that have been established after the development of the scorecard.

19. **Solution: d**
    a. Incorrect. The going concern assumption is that the business will have a long life. This does not relate directly to the practice of recording unearned revenues as liabilities.
    b. Incorrect. The monetary unit assumption is that money is the common denominator by which economic activity is conducted, and that the monetary unit provides an appropriate basis for accounting measurement and analysis. It does not relate directly to the practice of recording unearned revenues as liabilities.
    c. Incorrect. The historic cost principle is the requirement that most assets and liabilities be accounted for and reported on the basis of acquisition price. It does not relate directly to the practice of recording unearned revenues as liabilities.
    d. Correct. Since the amount received in cash has not yet been earned, it is appropriate to record the advance payment as a liability of the company. This is an example of the revenue recognition principle, which states that revenue should not be recognized until it is earned.

20. **Solution: d**
    a. Incorrect. There is no uncertainty regarding the amount of rent. Rent expense can be accrued as sales occur.
    b. Incorrect. A service was received and the company owes an amount. The amount is not contingent on a future event. The company can accrue the amount that it expected the invoice to show.
    c. Incorrect. As of the date of the interim financial statements, the income tax is payable because earnings have occurred. There is no uncertainty regarding the amount or the timing of the payment as of the date of the interim financial statements.
    d. Correct. This is a guarantee. The liability is contingent on the lessor not receiving the full residual value from a third party.

21. **Solution: c**
    a. Incorrect. Warranties are not a part of inventory valuation.
    b. Incorrect. Vendor pricing policies have no impact on inventory valuation until goods are purchased. The price at the time of purchase is the only price that matters in inventory valuation, and changes in vendor pricing policies would not necessarily impact valuation.
    c. Correct. The amount of inventory loss through shrinkage directly impacts inventory valuation. Inventory shrinkage must be considered in risk models involving inventory valuation.
    d. Incorrect. Sales forecasts do not affect inventory valuation.

22. **Solution: c**
    a. Incorrect. The balance of accumulated depreciation would be higher in the financial statements for tax purposes, since higher depreciation expense would be reported under accelerated depreciation than under straight-line depreciation.
    b. Incorrect. Depreciation expense is a non-cash charge. The cash balance is unaffected by the depreciation method used.
    c. Correct. Under accelerated depreciation, depreciation expense is higher and net income is lower. Retained earnings would therefore be lower for tax-reporting purposes than for general purpose financial reporting based on straight-line depreciation.
    d. Incorrect. The historic cost of fixed assets is recorded in the gross fixed assets account. The historic cost of the assets is unaffected by the depreciation method used.

23. **Solution: a**
    a. Correct. Under a defined contribution plan, the company reports an asset on the balance sheet only if the contribution to the pension trust is greater than the defined, required contribution.
    b. Incorrect. An asset is reported only if the contribution is in excess of the required contribution. If the actual contribution is equal to that required, no asset is reported.
    c. Incorrect. The company would report a liability on the balance sheet only if the contribution was less than the required amount, not greater than the required amount.
    d. Incorrect. The company would not report a liability on the balance sheet if it contributed the required amount to the pension trust.

24. **Solution: a**
    a. Correct. Leased assets are recognized as tangible assets. When lease agreements transfer the risks and benefits of ownership of the asset to the lessee, the lease is referred to as a capital lease since it is essentially a form of financing, or capital, for the lessee.
    b. Incorrect. Leased assets are not recognized as intangibles.
    c. Incorrect. If substantially all of the risks and benefits of ownership of the asset are transferred to the lessee, then the lease is referred to as a capital lease, not an operating lease.
    d. Incorrect. See answers "b" and "c".

25. **Solution: d**
    a. Incorrect. Income bonds only pay interest if interest is earned.
    b. Incorrect. Debentures are unsecured bonds.
    c. Incorrect. Subordinated debentures are subordinated to other debt.
    d. Correct. First-mortgage bonds are backed by fixed assets.

26. **Solution: a**
    a. Correct. Since the return to the U.S. company is adversely affected and the return to the European company is unaffected, the return to the U.S. company will definitely be lower than the return to the European company.
    b. Incorrect. The return to the U.S. company is adversely affected by the exchange rate movement.
    c. Incorrect. The return to the U.S. company is directly affected by the exchange rate movement, while the return to the European company is not.
    d. Incorrect. See answer "a".

27. Solution: d
   a. Incorrect. An offer that is "two-tier" involves two different offer prices for the shares acquired. The terms of the share acquisition do not relate to the issuance or repurchase of bonds in the company.
   b. Incorrect. See answer "a".
   c. Incorrect. This is the opposite of the correct answer.
   d. Correct. In a two-tier offer, shareholders are enticed to sell to the bidder early by a higher stock price offer for those who tender their stock earlier.

28. Solution: d
   a. Incorrect. The market value to book value ratio is the market value of common equity per share derived by dividing the book value of common equity by the average number of shares outstanding. Neither this ratio nor the total debt to total assets ratio provides any information about net income available to stockholders, which is necessary to calculate the return on equity.
   b. Incorrect. The price to earnings ratio is the ratio of the stock's market price divided by earnings per share; the earnings per share is the net income available to stockholders divided by the average number of shares outstanding; and the net profit margin is net profit divided by sales. While all three ratios contain much information about the equity account, none of them provides information about the book value of common equity, which is necessary to calculate the return on equity.
   c. Incorrect. The price to earnings ratio is the ratio of the stock's market price divided by earnings per share, and the return on assets ratio is net income divided by assets. Neither of these two ratios provides information about the book value of common equity, which is necessary to calculate the return on equity.
   d. Correct. These three ratios comprise the simple Du Pont equation:

   $$\frac{\text{Net Income Available to Stockholders}}{\text{Sales}} \times \frac{\text{Sales}}{\text{Total Assets}} \times \frac{\text{Total Assets}}{\text{Common Equity at Book Value}} = \text{Return on Equity}$$

   The total assets and sales cancel out in multiplication, leaving net income available to stockholders divided by common equity at book value, which equals return on equity.

29. Solution: c
   a. Incorrect. Inflation also distorts depreciation charges, inventory costs, and profits.
   b. Incorrect. Inflation impacts both aspects.
   c. Correct. Inflation impacts both aspects.
   d. Incorrect. Inflation impacts both aspects.

30. Solution: a
   a. Correct. The risk premium is the portion of expected return attributed to the increased risk.
   b. Incorrect. The coefficient of variation represents the standard deviation of an investment's returns divided by the mean returns.
   c. Incorrect. The standard error represents a measure of variability in the investment's returns.
   d. Incorrect. The beta coefficient represents the sensitivity of the investment's returns to the market returns.

31. Solution: b
   a. Incorrect. This answer ignores equity.
   b. Correct. Both debt and equity are factors in a company's capital structure.
   c. Incorrect. The decision does not directly involve assets.
   d. Incorrect. The decision involves equity, but does not focus on the type of equity used.

32. **Solution: a**
    a. Correct. Interest expense equals the carrying value of the liability at the beginning of the period times the effective interest rate. The carrying value of the liability equals the face value of the bond minus the discount. As the discount is amortized over the life of the bond, the carrying value increases. Consequently, the interest expense increases over the life of the bond.
    b. Incorrect. See answer "a".
    c. Incorrect. Interest expense exceeds the cash interest payment. The excess is the amount of discount amortized each period.
    d. Incorrect. See answer "c".

33. **Solution: a**
    a. Correct. In business terminology, a high degree of operating leverage, other things held constant, means that a relatively small change in sales will result in a large change in operating income. Therefore, if a high percentage of a firm's total cost is fixed, the firm is said to have a high degree of operating leverage.
    b. Incorrect. The opposite is true; see answer "a".
    c. Incorrect. See answer "a".
    d. Incorrect. See answer "a".

34. **Solution: a**
    a. Correct. The higher the dividend payout ratio, the sooner retained earnings are exhausted and the company must seek more costly, outside equity financing. This drives up the marginal cost of capital.
    b. Incorrect. The debt ratio is computed by dividing total debts by total assets. The dividend payout ratio has no impact on the debt ratio.
    c. Incorrect. The investment opportunities available to the company are not determined by the level of dividend payout.
    d. Incorrect. The opposite is true. The price to earnings ratio is computed by dividing price per share by earnings per share, so a company with a higher dividend payout ratio would have a lower price to earnings ratio.

35. **Solution: b**
    a. Incorrect. The cash balance maintained for making routine payments and collections is called the transactions balance.
    b. Correct. The cash balance called the compensating balance is the money left in a checking account in the bank in order to compensate the bank for services that it provides.
    c. Incorrect. The cash balance maintained as a reserve for unforeseen cash flow fluctuations is called the precautionary balance.
    d. Incorrect. It is the speculative cash balance that is maintained in order to enable the firm to take advantage of any bargain purchase opportunities that may arise.

36. **Solution: b**
    a. Incorrect. Securities prices are a good estimate of future cash flows under this theory.
    b. Correct. The market is continuously adjusting to new information and acting to correct pricing errors.
    c. Incorrect. Securities prices are the best benchmark under this theory.
    d. Incorrect. Securities prices equal their fair value as perceived by investors.

37. **Solution: c**
    a. Incorrect. A higher profit margin would reduce the additional financing needed, as stated in the question. The result would be a downward, not an upward, shift in the funds-needed line.
    b. Incorrect. See answer "a".
    c. Correct. A higher profit margin would reduce the additional financing needed, shifting the funds-needed line down.
    d. Incorrect. The line would become less, not more, steep if the firm had a higher profit margin.

38. **Solution: a**
    a. Correct. If all earnings are paid out as dividends, then there is no earnings retention. All sales growth must be financed from spontaneous or external sources.
    b. Incorrect. The funds-needed line only passes through the origin in the special case where all earnings are paid out as dividends.
    c. Incorrect. The funds-needed line is a graph of the relationship between sales growth rates and additional financing needs. It is not drawn for just one point, or one level of sales growth.
    d. Incorrect. While the sales growth rate would be zero at the point where the funds-needed line passed through the origin, funds needed may be non-zero when sales growth is zero.

39. **Solution: a**
    a. Correct. Under first-in, first-out (FIFO) inventory valuation, the 10,000 units in ending inventory are assumed to have been the most recent items purchased. The cost of the most recent 10,000 units purchased is:
    5,000 units @ $7.50 + 5,000 units @ $8 = $37,500 + $40,000 = $77,500.
    b. Incorrect. This solution is the ending inventory balance under the specific identification method if the units remaining in inventory at year end were identified as having been purchased on April 1 and July 1:
    5,000 units @ $9 + 5,000 units @ $8 = $45,000 + $40,000 = $85,000.
    c. Incorrect. This solution is the ending inventory balance under the average cost method. The average cost of all items purchased is used to calculate the ending inventory balance. The average cost of items purchased is:
    [$10 (5,000) + $9 (5,000) + $8 (5,000) + $7.50 (5,000)] / 20,000
    = $8.625 per unit so 10,000 units are assigned a value of $86,250.
    d. Incorrect. This solution is the ending inventory balance under the last-in, first-out (LIFO) method of inventory valuation. The most recent items purchased are assumed to be sold first, so the items remaining in inventory are assigned the cost of the earliest purchases:
    5,000 units @ $10 + 5,000 units @ $9 = $50,000 + $45,000 = $95,000.

40. **Solution: a**
    a. Correct. Under last-in, first-out (LIFO) inventory valuation, the 10,000 units sold during the year are assumed to have been those purchased most recently. The cost of goods sold for the year is calculated as:
    5,000 units @ $7.50 + 5,000 units @ $8 = $37,500 + $40,000 = $77,500.
    b. Incorrect. This is the solution if the average cost method is used. The average cost of all items purchased is $8.625 per unit so the 10,000 units sold are assigned a cost of $86,250.
    c. Incorrect. This is the solution if the specific identification method is used and if the units remaining in inventory at year end were identified as having been purchased on April 1 and July 1. The sold items would then have been purchased on January 1 and October 1, and cost of goods sold for the year is calculated as:
    5,000 units @ $10 + 5,000 units @ $7.50 = $50,000 + $37,500 = $87,500.
    d. Incorrect. This is the solution if the first-in, first-out (FIFO) method is used. Under FIFO, the oldest items are assumed to have been sold, so cost of goods sold for the year is calculated as:
    5,000 units @ $10 + 5,000 units @ $9 = $50,000 + $45,000 = $95,000.

41. Solution: a
a. Correct. The value of the firm is given by the expression:

$$V = \sum_{t=1}^{N} \frac{CF_t}{(1+k)^t}$$

where V is value, CF is net cash flow, k is the discount rate (cost of capital), and t is time. It follows that value will rise as CF increases.
b. Incorrect. An increase in systematic (or market) risk will increase the overall cost of capital and thereby increase K, the discount rate. As a result, the value of the firm will fall.
c. Incorrect. An increase in unsystematic (or firm-specific) risk is diversifiable and will have no affect on the value of the firm.
d. Incorrect. An increase in the discount rate will reduce the value of the firm.

42. Solution: d
a. Incorrect. Abnormal spoilage is not a function of the costing system; it is a function of the production process.
b. Incorrect. Abnormal spoilage may result from any of a variety of conditions or circumstances, which are generally controllable by first-line supervisors.
c. Incorrect. Abnormal spoilage may result from any of a variety of conditions or circumstances, which are not necessarily related to standards.
d. Correct. Abnormal spoilage is not expected under efficient operating conditions. It is not an inherent part of the production process.

43. Solution: b
a. Incorrect. Insurance on the corporate headquarters building is not a cost of production and is therefore a period cost.
b. Correct. Property taxes on a factory are a product cost.
c. Incorrect. Depreciation on salespersons' vehicles is not a cost of production and is therefore a period cost.
d. Incorrect. The salary of a sales manager is not a cost of production and is therefore a period cost.

44. Solution: b
a. Incorrect. This answer discounts the cash inflow at the correct discount rate (18%), but for four years instead of five, and also subtracts the cash inflow from the cash outflow, instead of vice versa.
b. Correct. The cash inflow at December 31 of year five is five years from the present cash outflow, and the net present value method uses the firm's cost of capital of 18%. The present value factor for 18% for five years is .4371, and $7,400,000 multiplied by .4371 equals $3,234,540, which is $265,460 less than the present cash outflow of $3,500,000.
c. Incorrect. This answer cannot be computed using the table values and dollar amounts given.
d. Incorrect. This answer discounts the cash inflow at the correct discount rate (18%), but for four years instead of five.

45. Solution: c
a. Incorrect. See answer "c".
b. Incorrect. See answer "c".
c. Correct. Twenty percent is the rate of return that equates the cash inflows with the cash outflows. The present value of 20 percent for five years is .4019, which multiplied by $9,950,000, equals $3,998,905. Therefore, the net present value of the project approximates $0 using the 20 percent rate.
d. Incorrect. See answer "c".

46. **Solution: a**
   a. Correct. This is the definition of a flexible budget.
   b. Incorrect. This is the definition of an operating budget.
   c. Incorrect. This is the definition of activity-based budgeting.
   d. Incorrect. This is the definition of Kaizen budgeting.

47. **Solution: c**
   a. Incorrect. Country X has a higher tax rate than the home country and country Y has a lower tax rate. The transfer pricing incentives will be different for the two sales divisions.
   b. Incorrect. See answer "a".
   c. Correct. Country X has a higher tax rate than the home country, so the incentive is to transfer profits out of country X. The sales division in country X will be less profitable if it is charged a high transfer price.
   d. Incorrect. Country Y has a lower tax rate than the home country, so the incentive is to transfer profits into country Y by charging that sales division a low transfer price.

48. **Solution: d**
   a. Incorrect. The master budget does not contain actual results.
   b. Incorrect. The master budget reflects all applicable expected costs, whether controllable by individual managers or not.
   c. Incorrect. The master budget is not structured to allow determination of manufacturing cost variances. This is accomplished using the flexible budget and actual results.
   d. Correct. The operating budget is a major element of the master budget.

49. **Solution: b**
   a. Incorrect. This answer only takes into account the rework cost and excludes the income that was lost when the units were sold as factory seconds: $12 x 1,200 = 14,400.
   b. Correct. This answer correctly includes both the cost of rework and the income lost when units were sold as factory seconds rather then first-quality units: [$12 + ($50 - $45)] x 1,200 = 20,400.
   c. Incorrect. This answer computes what the contribution margin would have been if the reworked items had been sold as first-quality units: [$50 - ($20 + $12)] x 1,200 = 21,600.
   d. Incorrect. This answer incorrectly computes the contribution margin for the reworked units, ignoring the $20 variable costs per unit. ($45 - $12) x 1,200 = 39,600.

50. **Solution: c**
   a. Incorrect. This is 80 percent of the actual sales, calculated as .80 ($2,000,000) = $1,600,000.
   b. Incorrect. This is the actual sales.
   c. Correct. Full capacity sales can be calculated as follows:
      Actual sales / Percent of capacity at which fixed assets were operated
      = $2,000,000/.80
      = $2,500,000.
   d. Incorrect. This is actual sales divided by the proportion of unused, rather than used, capacity, or $2,000,000/.2 = $10,000,000.

51. **Solution: a**
   a. Correct. Cost accumulation is performed by accounting systems that organize data by an appropriate catalog. Actual costs, rather than predicted costs, are accumulated.
   b. Incorrect. Computing depreciation expense would not organize data into categories.
   c. Incorrect. Producing financial statements would not organize data into categories.
   d. Incorrect. Forecasting material shortages would not organize data into categories.

52. Solution: d
   a. Incorrect. Process costing does not allocate costs per packing line. ($150,000 + 90,000 + 30,000 + 15,000 + 3,000 + 66,000 = $354,000/600,000 = .59/3 = $0.197).
   b. Incorrect. Process costing includes all costs. ($150,000 + 15,000 = 165,000/600,000 = $0.275).
   c. Incorrect. Process costing includes all costs. ($90,000 + 30,000 + 3,000 + 66,000 = 189,000/600,000 = $0.315).
   d. Correct. Process costing is the average cost per unit produced, or total cost divided by the number of units. ($150,000 + 90,000 + 30,000 + 15,000 + 3,000 + 66,000 = $354,000/600,000 = $0.59).

53. Solution: b
   a. Incorrect. This allocation basis is related to batch costs and not to individual unit costs.
   b. Correct. There is a direct causal relationship between the number of components in a finished product and the amount of material handling costs incurred.
   c. Incorrect. This allocation basis is the traditional basis for allocating overhead costs to the units produced when the production process is labor-intensive.
   d. Incorrect. This is not an allocation basis but rather the result of the allocation process when determining product costs.

54. Solution: b
   a. Incorrect. This is incorrect because both measures represent the results for a single time period.
   b. Correct. Residual income concentrates on earnings in excess of the minimum desired return. With ROI, a segment may reject a project that exceeds the minimum return if the project will decrease the segments overall ROI. For example, a project that earns ROI of 22%, which is greater than the target rate of 20%, might be rejected if the segment is currently earning 25%, because the project will decrease the segment's ROI. This would not occur with residual income.
   c. Incorrect. This is not correct because the target rate for ROI is the same as the imputed interest rate used in the residual income calculation.
   d. Incorrect. This is incorrect because average investment should be employed in both methods. At any rate, the investment base employed for both methods would be the same.

55. Solution: d
   a. Incorrect. Incremental costs are relevant if they occur in the future.
   b. Incorrect. Opportunity costs (benefits foregone) are relevant if they occur in the future.
   c. Incorrect. Outlay costs are relevant if they occur in the future.
   d. Correct. Sunk costs are always irrelevant because they occurred in the past.

56. Solution: a
   a. Correct. Selling government securities is contractional because it takes money out of circulation.
   b. Incorrect. Lower reserve requirements would fuel the economy because banks could lend more money.
   c. Incorrect. Lower discount rates would fuel the economy because borrowing would be encouraged.
   d. Incorrect. This is fiscal policy, not monetary policy.

57. Solution: d
   a. Incorrect. See answer "d".
   b. Incorrect. See answer "d".
   c. Incorrect. See answer "d".
   d. Correct. With trade quotas, home jobs will be saved; hence, unemployment will decline. Since jobs will be saved for inefficient industries (less efficient than foreign competitors), productivity rates will decline because they will not be specializing in those goods with which they have a comparative advantage.

58. Solution: a
    a. Correct. Investment tax credits are deductions from the corporate tax bill. The result is a lower investment cost and higher project net present values, all else equal.
    b. Incorrect. Tax credits are deductions from the actual corporate tax bill, and since more of profits are available for dividends, inflation would not be restrained.
    c. Incorrect. The opposite is true.
    d. Incorrect. Investment tax credits are not taxes levied on projects.

59. Solution: b
    a. Incorrect. See answer "b".
    b. Correct. Revenue tariffs are usually applied to products that are not produced domestically. Their purpose is to provide the government with tax revenues.
    c. Incorrect. Import quotas are designed to restrict the amount of a commodity that can be imported in a period of time.
    d. Incorrect. Voluntary export restrictions, which have the same effect as import quotas, encourage foreign firms to limit their exports to a particular country.

60. Solution: c
    a. Incorrect. Cost-reimbursable contracts are used when the requirements are complex and costs cannot be easily identified and estimated.
    b. Incorrect. Indefinite delivery contracts are used only when the supplies and/or service of future deliveries are not known at the time of contract award.
    c. Correct. Fixed-price contracts are used when the requirements are well-defined, uncertainties can be identified and costs estimated, and there is adequate competition.
    d. Incorrect. Time-and-materials contracts are used when it is not possible at the time of placing the contract to estimate accurately the duration of the work.

61. Solution: c
    a. Incorrect. Progressive taxes, for which the average tax rate rises as income rises, take both a larger percentage of income and a larger absolute amount of income as income rises.
    b. Incorrect. Proportional taxes, for which the average tax rate is constant for all income levels, always take a larger absolute amount of income as income rises.
    c. Correct. Regressive taxes are those for which the average tax rate falls as income rises. They take a smaller percentage of income as income rises, so they will not necessarily take a larger absolute amount of income as income rises.
    d. Incorrect. A flat tax would have the same percentage tax rate regardless of income and would therefore take a larger absolute amount of income as income rises.

62. Solution: c
    a. Incorrect. It is temporary differences that result in taxable or deductible amounts in some future year(s), when the reported amounts of assets are recovered and the reported amounts of liabilities are settled.
    b. Incorrect. Temporary differences have deferred tax consequences while the permanent differences do not. Permanent differences affect only the period in which they occur.
    c. Correct. Permanent differences have no deferred tax consequences because they affect only the period in which they occur. Permanent differences include (1) items that enter into pre-tax financial income but never into taxable income and (2) items that enter into taxable income but never into pre-tax financial income. In contrast, temporary differences result in taxable or deductible amounts in some future year(s), when the reported amounts of assets are recovered and the reported amounts of liabilities are settled. Temporary differences therefore do have deferred tax consequences while permanent differences do not.
    d. Incorrect. Permanent differences, not temporary differences, include items that enter into pre-tax financial income but never into taxable income.

63. Solution: a
   a. Correct. A value-added tax is collected on the basis of the value created by the firm. This is measured as the difference between the value of its outputs and its inputs.
   b. Incorrect. This is a description of how to calculate capital gains tax.
   c. Incorrect. This is a description of an internal transfer price.
   d. Incorrect. This is a description of how to calculate income tax.

64. Solution: b
   a. Incorrect. By definition, gross national product (GNP) = C + I + G + X, where C is consumption, I is investment, G is government, and X is net exports (exports minus imports). Therefore, GNP will rise with an increase in consumption.
   b. Correct. A rise in imports will cause a fall in net exports and GNP.
   c. Incorrect. An increase in exports will increase GNP.
   d. Incorrect. An increase in inflation will increase GNP.

65. Solution: b
   a. Incorrect. Review of the computer processing logs is an output control to ensure that data are accurate and complete.
   b. Correct. Matching the input data with information held on master or suspense files is a processing control, not an output control, to ensure that data are complete and accurate during updating.
   c. Incorrect. Periodic reconciliation of output reports is an output control to ensure that data are accurate and complete.
   d. Incorrect. Maintaining formal procedures and documentation specifying authorized recipients is an output control to ensure proper distribution.

66. Solution: c
   a. Incorrect. Frequently, the purpose of database reviews is to determine if: (1) users have gained access to database areas for which they have no authorization, and (2) authorized users can access the database using programs that provide them with unauthorized privileges to view and/or change information.
   b. Incorrect. The purpose of compliance reviews is to determine whether an organization has complied with applicable internal and external procedures and regulations.
   c. Correct. Program change control comprises: (1) maintaining records of change authorizations, code changes, and test results; (2) adhering to a systems development methodology (including documentation); (3) authorizing changeovers of subsidiary and headquarters' interfaces; and (4) restricting access to authorized source and executable codes.
   d. Incorrect. The purpose of network security software is to provide logical controls over the network.

67. Solution: c
   a. Incorrect. Programmed cutoff controls mitigate the risk of recording transactions in the wrong period.
   b. Incorrect. Redundant hardware is a control over hardware malfunction.
   c. Correct. Activity logging provides an audit trail of user activity.
   d. Incorrect. Transaction error logging controls transactions rather than user terminal activity.

68. Solution: c
   a. Incorrect. Legibility of image data is important to its use, but is independent of using the wrong image.
   b. Incorrect. Accuracy of image data is important to its use, but is independent of using the wrong image.
   c. Correct. If index data for image processing systems are corrupted, users will likely be relying on the wrong images.
   d. Incorrect. Maintaining the initial sequence of index data may not be possible as the image data is modified and images are added/dropped.

69. **Solution: a**
   a. Correct. Implementation controls occur in the systems development process at various points to ensure that implementation is properly controlled and managed.
   b. Incorrect. Hardware controls ensure that computer hardware is physically secure and check for equipment malfunction.
   c. Incorrect. Computer operations controls apply to the work of the computer department and help ensure that programmed procedures are consistently and correctly applied to the storage and processing of data.
   d. Incorrect. Data security controls ensure that data files on either disk or tape are not subject to unauthorized access, change, or destruction.

70. **Solution: a**
   a. Correct. A gateway, often implemented via software, translates between two or more different protocol families and makes connections between dissimilar networks possible.
   b. Incorrect. A bridge joins network segments so that they appear to be one physical segment.
   c. Incorrect. A router connects two or more network segments, such that the segments maintain their separate logical identities.
   d. Incorrect. A wiring concentrator accepts twisted-pair cabling from each of several personal computers in the same local area network.

71. **Solution: b**
   a. Incorrect. Exception reporting can be used to control correctness and timeliness of updates but cannot minimize the impact of an interruption.
   b. Correct. The capability to continue processing at all sites except a nonfunctioning one is called fail-soft protection, an advantage of distributed systems.
   c. Incorrect. Backup procedures are intended to prevent the recovery process from introducing any erroneous changes into the system after computer failure.
   d. Incorrect. Data file security is intended to prevent unauthorized changes to data files.

72. **Solution: b**
   a. Incorrect. See answer "b".
   b. Correct. A check digit is an extra reference number that follows an identification code and bears a mathematical relationship to the other digits. This extra digit is input with the data. The identification code can be subjected to an algorithm and compared to the check digit.
   c. Incorrect. See answer "b".
   d. Incorrect. See answer "b".

73. **Solution: a**
   a. Correct. Marked benefits come about when EDI is tied to strategic efforts that alter, not mirror, previous practices. Applying EDI to an inefficient process results in the ability to continue doing things wrong, only faster.
   b. Incorrect. The prerequisite for EDI success is an understanding of the mission of the business and the processes and flows that support its goals, followed by cooperation with external partners. Hardware concerns come later.
   c. Incorrect. Before applying EDI technology to the business, EDI must be viewed as part of an overall integrated solution to organizational requirements.
   d. Incorrect. EDI is not a solution by itself. Instead of thinking about how to send transactions back and forth, a company has to first think about the entire process from both ends.

74. **Solution: b**
   a. Incorrect. To address this issue, unauthorized access to the EDI system should be prevented, procedures should be in place to ensure the effective use of passwords, and data integrity and privacy should be maintained through the use of encryption and authentication measures.
   b. Correct. Tracking of customers' functional acknowledgments, when required, will help to ensure successful transmission of EDI transactions.
   c. Incorrect. Contractual agreements should exist between the company and the EDI trading partners.
   d. Incorrect. The risk that EDI data may not be completely and accurately processed is primarily controlled by the system.

75. **Solution: d**
   a. Incorrect. See answer "d".
   b. Incorrect. See answer "d".
   c. Incorrect. See answer "d".
   d. Correct. With a format check, the computer checks the characteristics of the character content, length, or sign of the individual data fields.

76. **Solution: c**
   a. Incorrect. Write-once-read-many (WORM) is an optical storage technique often used as an archival medium.
   b. Incorrect. Digital audiotape (DAT) is primarily used as a backup medium in imaging systems and as a master for CD-ROM.
   c. Correct. Compact-disc/read-only memory (CD-ROM) would be cheaper to produce and ship than the existing paper yet permit large volumes of text and images to be reproduced. Users of the electronic equipment are likely to have access to CD-ROM readers on personal computers so that they could use the documentation on CD-ROM.
   d. Incorrect. Computer-output-to-microform (COM) is used for frequent access to archived documents such as canceled checks in banking applications.

77. **Solution: d**
   a. Incorrect. Application audits should be about the same difficulty with or without an adequately staffed help desk.
   b. Incorrect. Preparation of documentation is a development function, not a help desk function.
   c. Incorrect. The likelihood of use of unauthorized program code is a function of change control, not of a help desk.
   d. Correct. The biggest risk in not having an adequately staffed help desk is that users will unknowingly persist in making errors in their interaction with the information systems.

78. **Solution: a**
   a. Correct. Optical character recognition (OCR) software converts images of paper documents, as read by a scanning device, into text document computer files.
   b. Incorrect. See answer "a".
   c. Incorrect. See answer "a".
   d. Incorrect. See answer "a".

79. **Solution: a**
   a. Correct. Internally encrypted passwords are controls designed to preclude users browsing the password file with a utility software application.
   b. Incorrect. A password hierarchy represents a set of interrelated authorization codes to distinguish between action privileges such as reading, adding, or deleting records.
   c. Incorrect. Logon passwords represent the initial user authorization access codes to the typical system.
   d. Incorrect. A peer-to-peer network is a system, which relies on a series of equal microcomputers for processing.

80. Solution: c
    a. Incorrect. A logic bomb is a mechanism for releasing a system attack of some kind, which is triggered when a particular condition (for example, a certain date or system operation) occurs.
    b. Incorrect. A virus is a code fragment (not an independent program) that reproduces by attaching to another program.
    c. Correct. A worm is an independent program that reproduces by copying itself from one system to another over a network and consumes computer and network resources.
    d. Incorrect. A Trojan horse is an independent program that appears to perform a useful function, but hides another unauthorized program inside it.

81. Solution: d
    a. Incorrect. Key verification ensures the accuracy of selected fields by requiring a different individual to re-key them.
    b. Incorrect. Sequence checks are used to ensure the completeness of input or update data by checking the use of pre-assigned document serial numbers.
    c. Incorrect. Computer matching entails checking selected fields of input data with information held in a suspense or master file.
    d. Correct. Users can gain access to databases from terminals only through established recognition and authorization procedures; thus, unauthorized access is prevented.

82. Solution: c (I and III only)
    I. Correct. This is a true statement.
    II. Incorrect. A confidential mail message should not be retained on the server once the user has downloaded it to a personal computer.
    III. Correct. This is a true statement.

83. Solution: b
    a. Incorrect. Data encryption provides adequate security for notebook computers.
    b. Correct. Password protection for a screen-saver program can be easily bypassed.
    c. Incorrect. Removable hard drives would provide adequate security.
    d. Incorrect. Security is promoted by physically locking the notebook computer in a case.

84. Solution: a
    a. Correct. While most delete programs erase file pointers, they do not remove the underlying data. The company must use special utilities that fully erase the data. This is important because of the potential for confidential data on the microcomputers.
    b. Incorrect. This could create a liability for the company if a virus destroyed the purchasing party's data or programs. However, the purchasing party should use anti-virus software to detect and eliminate any viruses. This concern, while important, is not as serious as the one in answer "a".
    c. Incorrect. The purchasing party has a responsibility to insure that all their software is properly licensed. If the company represented that all the software was properly licensed, this could create a liability. However, this liability is not as serious as the implication from answer "a".
    d. Incorrect. Terminal emulation software is widely available.

85. Solution: c
    a. Incorrect. External risks should be evaluated to determine the center's location.
    b. Incorrect. Biometric access systems control physical access to the data center.
    c. Correct. Authorization tables for operating system access address logical controls, not physical controls.
    d. Incorrect. Power supply systems and surge protection are included in data center design.

86. Solution: c
    a. Incorrect. Contingency planning refers to the arrangements for alternative processing facilities in the event of equipment failure.
    b. Incorrect. The feasibility study is one of the phases in the systems development life cycle.
    c. Correct. The plan should include goals and objectives, an inventory of current capacity, and a forecast of future needs.
    d. Incorrect. Exception reports are meant to highlight problems and bring them to the attention of management.

87. Solution: c
    a. Incorrect. System documentation is not eliminated or deferred by using rapid application development.
    b. Incorrect. Project management involves development teams.
    c. Correct. The new system would be developed module by module.
    d. Incorrect. Object development might not be of use; if it were, it would increase usage of previous code.

88. Solution: a
    a. Correct. An expert system is a knowledge-intensive computer program that captures the expertise of a human in limited domains of knowledge.
    b. Incorrect. A neural network is software that attempts to emulate the processing patterns of the biological brain.
    c. Incorrect. Intelligent agents are software programs that use a built-in or learned knowledge base to carry out specific, repetitive, and predictable tasks for an individual user, business process, or software application. On the Internet, an intelligent agent is generally a program that gathers information or performs some other service without the user's immediate presence and on some regular schedule.
    d. Incorrect. Fuzzy logic is rule-based artificial intelligence that tolerates imprecision by using non-specific terms called membership functions to solve problems.

89. Solution: d
    a. Incorrect. Instead of traditional design documents, items such as the business model, narratives of process functions, iterative development screens, computer processes and reports, and product descriptions guides are produced in object-oriented development, but the existence of specific documents does not affect the importance of user acceptance testing.
    b. Incorrect. In general, object-oriented development systems do include tracking systems for changes made to objects and hierarchies.
    c. Incorrect. Because object-oriented systems are usually developed in client/server environments, there is the potential for continuous monitoring of system use, but continuous monitoring typically occurs during system operation, not during development.
    d. Correct. User acceptance testing is more important in object-oriented development because of the fact that all objects in a class inherit the properties of the hierarchy, which means that changes to one object may affect other objects, which increases the importance of user acceptance testing to verify correct functioning of the whole system.

90. Solution: d
    a. Incorrect. The absence of processing interruptions indicates nothing about the interruptions that might occur in the future, especially those that are not under the organization's control.
    b. Incorrect. A contingency plan may have comprehensive documentation, but until the plan is tested, an organization has no indication of its effectiveness.
    c. Incorrect. Audit signoff is one indicator of plan quality, but until the plan is tested, an organization has no indication of its effectiveness.
    d. Correct. The only way to know whether contingency planning has been effective is to test the plan, by simulating an interruption or by conducting a paper test with a walk-through of recovery procedures.

91. **Solution: c**
    a. Incorrect. This practice is a wise control, but it does not address the issue of the integrity of uploaded data. Backups cannot prevent or detect data-upload problems, but can only help correct data errors that a poor upload caused.
    b. Incorrect. This control may be somewhat helpful in preventing fraud in data uploads, but it is of little use in preventing errors.
    c. Correct. This could help prevent data errors.
    d. Incorrect. This control is detective in nature, but the error could have already caused erroneous reports and management decisions. Having users try to find errors in uploaded data would be costly.

92. **Solution: d**
    a. Incorrect. Physical controls limit access to an area and do not include passwords.
    b. Incorrect. Edit controls test the validity of data.
    c. Incorrect. Digital controls are examples of physical controls.
    d. Correct. Passwords are a form of access controls since they limit access to computer systems and the information stored in them.

93. **Solution: d**
    a. Incorrect. The reviews of jobs processed will disclose access, but will not prevent it.
    b. Incorrect. Comparison of production programs and controlled copies will disclose changes, but will not prevent them.
    c. Incorrect. Periodic running of test data will detect changes, but will not prevent them.
    d. Correct. When duties are separated, users cannot obtain a detailed knowledge of programs and computer operators cannot gain unsupervised access to production programs.

94. **Solution: d**
    a. Incorrect. Asynchronous modems handle data streams from peripheral devices to a central processor.
    b. Incorrect. Authentication techniques confirm that valid users have access to the system.
    c. Incorrect. Call-back procedures are used to ensure incoming calls are from authorized locations.
    d. Correct. Cryptographic devices protect data in transmission over communication lines.

95. **Solution: d**
    a. Incorrect. Data terminals do not normally use screen-saver protection.
    b. Incorrect. Scripting is the use of a program to automate a process such as startup.
    c. Incorrect. Encryption of data files will not prevent the viewing of data on an unattended data terminal.
    d. Correct. Automatic log-off of inactive users may prevent the viewing of sensitive data on an unattended data terminal.

96. **Solution: a**
    a. Correct. Users need to update data through applications programs.
    b. Incorrect. Application programmers should not be able to change production programs. They should submit changes to the change control unit.
    c. Incorrect. Application programmers should never have update access to production data. Users have no need to change production programs.
    d. Incorrect. See answers "b" and "c".

97. **Solution: c**
   a. Incorrect. Installing a logging system for program access would permit detection of unauthorized access but would not prevent it.
   b. Incorrect. Monitoring physical access to program library media would control only unauthorized physical access.
   c. Correct. Restricting physical and logical access secures program libraries from unauthorized use, in person and remotely via terminals.
   d. Incorrect. Denying all remote access via terminals would likely be inefficient and would not secure program libraries against physical access.

98. **Solution: a**
   a. Correct. Data definition language (DDL) is used to define (that is, determine) the database.
   b. Incorrect. Data control language (DCL) is used to specify privileges and security rules.
   c. Incorrect. Data manipulation language (DML) provides programmers with a facility to update the database.
   d. Incorrect. Data query language (DQL) is used for ad hoc queries.

99. **Solution: c**
   a. Incorrect. Most query tools include the capability of presenting the results of queries graphically.
   b. Incorrect. Query tools include data dictionary access because that is how they know what table attributes to present to users.
   c. Correct. The least likely feature of a query tool would be a data validity checker because the database system has already enforced any validity constraints at the time the data were inserted in the database. Any further data validity checking would be a function of a user application program rather than a query.
   d. Incorrect. Query tools typically have a query-by-example interface.

100. **Solution: b**
   a. Incorrect. There is no limitation on the number of access ports.
   b. Correct. The most difficult aspect of using Internet resources is locating the best information given the large number of information sources.
   c. Incorrect. The only equipment required for accessing Internet resources is a computer, a modem, a telephone or other access line, and basic communication software.
   d. Incorrect. Organizations routinely provide Internet access to their employees, and individuals can obtain access through individual subscriptions to commercial service providers.

END OF PART III SOLUTIONS

Certified Internal Auditor (CIA) Model Exam Questions

Part IV - Business Management Skills

Part IV Model Exam Questions: 100

Questions on actual CIA Exam Part IV: 125
(see explanation in "Foreword" on page iii)

Time allowed for completion of CIA Exam Part IV: 210 minutes

Instructions such as those that follow will be listed on the cover of each CIA examination. Please read them carefully.

1. Place your candidate number on the answer sheet in the space provided.
2. Do not place extraneous marks on the answer sheet.
3. Be certain that changes to answers are **completely** erased.
4. All references to the *Professional Practices Framework* refer to The IIA's *Professional Practices Framework*, which includes the *Standards* and the *Practice Advisories*. All references to *Standards* refer to the *International Standards for the Professional Practice of Internal Auditing* outlined in The IIA's *Professional Practices Framework*.

Failure to follow these instructions and the "Instructions to Candidates" guidelines could adversely affect both your right to receive the results of this examination and your future participation in the Certified Internal Auditor program.

All papers submitted in completion of any part of this examination become the sole property of The Institute of Internal Auditors, Inc. Candidates may not disclose the contents of this exam unless expressly authorized by the Certification Department.

1. When firms compete in different geographical locations or have multiple product lines that do not necessarily overlap, the most effective way of responding to an aggressive move by a competitor without directly triggering destructive moves and countermoves is to:
   a. Mislead the competitor into taking or not taking an action.
   b. Make a prior announcement of intended moves.
   c. Initiate a move in the market where the competitor is strong.
   d. Initiate direct aggressive moves.

2. The key component of an organization configured as a professional bureaucracy is the:
   a. Strategic apex.
   b. Technostructure.
   c. Line administration.
   d. Operating core.

3. A manufacturing company produces plastic utensils for a particular market segment at the lowest possible cost. The company is pursuing a cost:
   a. Leadership strategy.
   b. Focus strategy.
   c. Differentiation strategy.
   d. Containment strategy.

4. The concurrent action of basic competitive forces as defined by Porter's model determines the:
   a. Long-term profitability and the competency intensity of the industry.
   b. Barriers that potential players must face to enter the industry.
   c. Rivalry within the industry.
   d. Strategy that a company should follow to achieve its objectives.

5. Which of the following is a market-oriented definition of a business versus a product-oriented definition of a business?
   a. We make air conditioners and furnaces.
   b. We supply energy.
   c. We produce movies.
   d. We sell clothing.

6. Which of the following statements best describes a market synergy?
   a. Technology transfer from one product to another.
   b. Bundling of products distributed through the same channels.
   c. Production of multiple products at one facility.
   d. Use of complementary management skills to achieve entry into a new market

7. Which of the following is a strategy that companies can use to stimulate innovation?
   I. Source from the most advanced suppliers.
   II. Establish employee programs that reward initiative.
   III. Identify best practice competitors as motivators.
   IV. Ensure that performance targets are always achieved.

   a. I only.
   b. II and IV only.
   c. I, II, and III only.
   d. I, II, III, and IV.

8. Which of the following is a basic force that drives industry competition and which, when combined with other competitive forces, determines the ultimate profit potential in the industry?
   I. Threat of new entrants.
   II. Bargaining power of suppliers.
   III. Favorable access to raw materials.
   IV. Product differentiation.

   a. I only.
   b. I and II only.
   c. III and IV only.
   d. I, II, III, and IV.

9. Which of the following is **not** characteristic of a mature industry environment?
   a. Consolidation.
   b. Competitive interdependence.
   c. Falling demand.
   d. Strategic focus on deterring entry of new competitors into the marketplace.

10. In which of the following industry environments are franchising and horizontal mergers commonly used strategies?
    a. Emerging industries.
    b. Declining industries.
    c. Fragmented industries.
    d. Mature industries.

11. Which of the following costs does management need to consider when introducing a new product or substituting a new product for an existing one?

    I. Costs of retraining employees.
    II. Costs of acquiring new ancillary equipment.
    III. Write-offs due to undepreciated investment in old technology.
    IV. Capital requirements for changeover.

    a. I and III only.
    b. I, II, and IV only.
    c. II, III, and IV only.
    d. I, II, III, and IV.

12. Which of the following would be a source of global competitive advantage?
    a. Low fixed costs.
    b. Production economies of scale.
    c. Weak copyright protection.
    d. Intensive local service requirements.

13. Governments restrict trade in order to:

    I. Foster national security.
    II. Develop new industries.
    III. Protect declining industries.
    IV. Increase tax revenues.

    a. I and IV only.
    b. II and III only.
    c. I, II, and III only.
    d. II, III, and IV only.

14. Which of the following is a social trend affecting an organization?
    a. Changes in the labor markets.
    b. Tougher legislation to protect the environment.
    c. Rising inflation.
    d. Replacements for steel in cars and appliances.

15. Which of the following factors would encourage entry into an existing market?
    a. Governmental subsidy for new investors
    b. High product differentiation, principally produced by trademarks
    c. Knowledge of the industry, with high investments in development
    d. Low exit fixed costs

16. A backward integration strategy is most appropriate when the firm's current suppliers are:
    a. Highly reliable.
    b. Not reliable.
    c. Geographically dispersed.
    d. Geographically concentrated.

17. Just-in-time production:
    a. Reduces the dependency on suppliers.
    b. Reduces the cost of implementing new strategies.
    c. Decreases production facility flexibility.
    d. Increases the need for a dependable workforce.

18. The opportunity for franchising comes from the ability to:
    a. Develop products.
    b. Differentiate products.
    c. Standardize products.
    d. Diversify products.

19. Capacity expansion is also referred to as:
    a. Market penetration.
    b. Market development.
    c. Product development.
    d. Diversification.

20. A milk-producing company acquires its own dairy farms to supply milk. The growth strategy adopted by the company can be identified as:
    a. Horizontal integration.
    b. Vertical integration.
    c. Concentric diversification.
    d. Conglomerate diversification.

21. A firm has a strategic business unit (SBU) that has a low market share in a high growth market. To maintain even this low share of the market requires the firm to commit a significant amount of cash. The firm might successfully adopt a build strategy for this unit if the:

    I. SBU shows a strong potential to grow and obtains a significant share of the market.
    II. Firm can finance its growth.
    III. Firm expects a short-term increase in cash flow.
    IV. Firm is willing to forego short-term earnings.

    a. I only.
    b. II and III only.
    c. III and IV only.
    d. I, II, and IV only.

22. Which of the following statements is true regarding organizational objectives?
    a. Objectives are not needed in order to set targets and direction.
    b. Objective setting is often a result of negotiation.
    c. Objectives are general statements of direction in line with a goal.
    d. Objectives need not be continually updated to reflect environmental changes.

23. In the Boston Consulting Group (BCG) growth-share matrix, which strategy in the matrix describes large generation of cash and heavy investment needed to grow and maintain competitive positioning but net cash flow is usually modest?
    a. Cash cows.
    b. Question marks.
    c. Dogs.
    d. Stars.

24. In the product life cycle, the first symptom of the decline stage is a decline in a:
    a. Firm's inventory levels.
    b. Product's sales.
    c. Product's production cost.
    d. Product's prices.

25. During the growth stage of the product life cycle:
    a. Quality of products is poor.
    b. Quality of products continuously improves.
    c. There is little difference between competing products.
    d. Quality of products becomes more variable and products are less differentiated.

26. During the introduction stage of an innovative product, sales growth is normally slow due to:
    a. Expensive sales promotion.
    b. High competition.
    c. Overproduction.
    d. Available alternatives.

27. The price charged on a consistent basis for a specific product would most likely be lowest during which stage of the product life cycle?
    a. Introduction stage.
    b. Growth stage.
    c. Maturity stage.
    d. Decline stage.

28. The opportunity for cost reductions would be greatest in which stage of the product life cycle?
    a. Introduction stage.
    b. Growth stage.
    c. Maturity stage.
    d. Decline stage.

29. Which of the following is the most significant reason that domestic governments and international organizations seek to eliminate cartels?
    a. Increased sales prices reduce the amount of corporate tax revenues payable to the government.
    b. True competition keeps prices as low as possible, thus increasing efficiency in the marketplace.
    c. Small businesses cannot survive or grow without government protection.
    d. The economic stability of developing countries depends on a global free market.

30. When a multinational firm decides to sell its products abroad, one of the risks that it faces is that the government of the foreign market could charge the firm with dumping, which occurs when:
    a. A product sells at different prices geographically.
    b. A firm charges less than it costs to make a product in order to enter and win market share.
    c. Lower quality versions of a product are sold abroad in order to be affordable.
    d. Transfer prices are set artificially high in order to minimize tax payments.

31. When initiating international ventures, an organization should consider cultural dimensions to prevent misunderstandings. Which of the following does **not** represent a recognized cultural dimension in a work environment?
    a. Self-control.
    b. Power distance.
    c. Masculinity versus femininity.
    d. Uncertainty avoidance.

32. Which of the following would increase understanding of a complex and ambiguous situation confronted by an organization?

    I. Brainstorming.
    II. Polling.
    III. Lateral thinking.

    a. I only.
    b. I and III only.
    c. II and III only.
    d. I, II, and III.

33. Which of the following represents the most significant impediment to merging customer databases across international boundaries?
    a. Response time.
    b. Taxation issues.
    c. Privacy regulations.
    d. Backup and recovery.

34. The three major factors favoring globalization are:
    a. Cultural, commercial, technical.
    b. Flexibility, proximity, adaptability.
    c. Political, technological, social.
    d. Ambition, positioning, organization.

35. Which of the following management orientations is characterized by an organization's efforts to adapt the product and marketing program to each local environment?
    a. Ethnocentric.
    b. Polycentric.
    c. Geocentric.
    d. Regiocentric.

36. Globalization assists in achieving economies of scale, which is a:
    a. Cost benefit.
    b. Timing benefit.
    c. Learning benefit.
    d. Arbitrage benefit.

37. In some regions of the world, business is conducted more often through personal relationship building than through legal contracts. This is an example of a:
    a. Cultural factor.
    b. Commercial factor.
    c. Technical factor.
    d. Legal factor.

38. Multinational companies are better poised to manage their overseas tax liability by:
    a. Declaring lower profits in countries with lower taxation levels.
    b. Declaring higher profits in countries with lower taxation levels.
    c. Charging higher prices for components in countries with lower taxation levels.
    d. Charging lower prices for components in countries with higher taxation levels.

39. Which of the following describes a source of communication breakdown which occurs within an organization due to a sense of superiority by members of a particular culture over another?
    a. Perceptual problem.
    b. Stereotyping.
    c. Ethnocentrism.
    d. Uncertainty avoidance.

40. Nationalism, expropriation, and terrorism are best categorized as examples of:
    a. Economic risk.
    b. Political risk.
    c. Operational risk.
    d. Environmental risk.

41. Which of the following is a cultural aspect that typically makes international and intercultural communication more difficult?

    I. Long distances between sender and receiver.
    II. Body language.
    III. Language.
    IV. Attitude.
    V. Time.

    a. I and III only.
    b. II and V only.
    c. I, IV, and V only.
    d. II, III, IV, and V only.

42. Globalization and localization are shaping the competitive structure of industries. The scenario contributing to the most competitive environment is when:
    a. Global forces dominate.
    b. Local forces dominate.
    c. Mix of global and local forces dominate.
    d. Neither global nor local forces dominate.

43. For a multinational firm, which of the following is a **disadvantage** of an ethnocentric staffing policy in which all key management positions are filled by parent-company nationals?
    a. It significantly raises the compensation, training, and staffing costs.
    b. It produces resentment among the firm's employees in host countries.
    c. It limits career mobility for parent-country nationals.
    d. It isolates headquarters from foreign subsidiaries.

44. One of the keys to successfully redesigning jobs is:
    a. Creating autonomous work teams.
    b. Enlarging jobs by adding more tasks similar to those being performed.
    c. Rotating workers to different jobs to provide them with variety.
    d. Changing the content of jobs so that they fit workers' need for growth.

45. An employee's need for self-actualization would be met by:
    a. Attractive pension provisions.
    b. Challenging new job assignments.
    c. Good working conditions.
    d. Regular positive feedback.

46. Which of the following theories includes the assertion that employees may be motivated by achievement of acceptance or esteem in the workplace?
    a. Equity theory.
    b. Expectancy theory.
    c. Needs hierarchy theory.
    d. Goal-setting theory.

47. Which of the following actions taken by management would **not** be effective in motivating an employee to superior performance?
    a. Job enlargement.
    b. Job enrichment.
    c. Job security.
    d. Job rotation.

48. Which of the following strengthens and increases acceptable behavior by termination or withdrawal of undesirable consequences?
    a. Positive reinforcement.
    b. Negative reinforcement.
    c. Reward.
    d. Punishment.

49. Among the nonfinancial rewards to an employee, a paid vacation trip can best be categorized as:
    a. Social reward.
    b. Token award.
    c. Visual/auditory reward.
    d. Manipulatables.

50. Cross-training of employees in various functions is an example of job:
    a. Enlargement.
    b. Rotation.
    c. Enrichment.
    d. Redesign.

51. Which of the following is a management approach to motivating employees?

    I. Providing performance feedback.
    II. Presenting opportunities for responsibility.
    III. Satisfying personal needs.

    a. III only.
    b. I and II only.
    c. II and III only.
    d. I, II, and III.

52. Which of the following is an example of choosing which information is to be presented in order to ensure that the presenter is seen in the best possible light?
    a. Filtering.
    b. Selective perception.
    c. Emotion.
    d. Language choice.

53. Which of the following is an effective active listening technique?

    I. Summarizing.
    II. Clarifying.
    III. Evaluating.
    IV. Empathizing

    a. I and IV only.
    b. II and III only.
    c. I, II, and IV only.
    d. I, II, III, and IV.

54. Which of the following steps works against effective listening?
    a. Listening for the emotion in the situation.
    b. Asking good questions.
    c. Listening to the steps to reach a solution.
    d. Helping the speaker to complete the point.

55. Job instructions, official memos, and procedures manuals are examples of which type of organizational communication?
    a. Upward.
    b. Downward.
    c. Lateral.
    d. Diagonal.

56. Which of the following is considered a **disadvantage** of electronic communication?

    I. Information overload.
    II. Misrepresentation of feelings and emotions.
    III. Reduced transmission time.
    IV. Lack of paper trail.

    a. I and II only.
    b. II and IV only.
    c. I, II, and III only.
    d. I, II, III, and IV.

57. Which of the following is the best measure of productivity to use to evaluate several departments in a large retail store?
    a. Number of customers served per employee per day.
    b. Revenue per square foot.
    c. Number of units sold per department per day.
    d. Average number of units stocked per month per department.

58. After three years of steadily decreasing profits in spite of increased sales and a growing economy, which of the following is the preferred course of action for a chief executive officer to take?
    a. Set a turnaround goal of significantly increasing profits within two months.
    b. Reduce staff by 10 percent in every unit.
    c. Reduce staff in the nonvalue-adding functions by 20 percent.
    d. Encourage innovation at all levels and use an early retirement program to reduce staff size.

59. Which of the following is an example of an efficiency measure?
    a. The rate of absenteeism.
    b. The goal of becoming a leading manufacturer.
    c. The number of insurance claims processed per day.
    d. The rate of customer complaints.

60. The alignment of managerial goals with organizational goals usually requires:

    I. Assigning responsibility for activities.
    II. Delegating the authority to perform necessary tasks.
    III. Establishing accountability.
    IV. Measuring and evaluating performance.

    a. I and IV only.
    b. I, II, and III only.
    c. II, III, and IV only.
    d. I, II, III, and IV.

61. Which of the following is generally true regarding a manager's span of control?
    a. Narrow spans of control are typically found in flat organizations, which have few hierarchical levels.
    b. An organization with narrow spans of control needs more managers than one with wider spans of control.
    c. Wider spans of control mean higher administrative expense and less self-management.
    d. Wider spans of control help ensure good internal controls and policy compliance throughout an organization.

62. In which of the following situations would a narrower span of control be more appropriate?
    a. Managers do not spend a great deal of time on planning or strategic management.
    b. Managers must spend a great deal of time coordinating with other managers.
    c. Subordinates work in the same area, rather than being geographically dispersed.
    d. Work performed by subordinates is substantially identical.

63. A 360-degree performance appraisal typically requires inputs from:

   I. Employees who are subordinates.
   II. Employees in other business units.
   III. Peers and teammates.
   IV. Customer satisfaction data.

   a. I and IV only.
   b. I, II, and III only.
   c. II, III, and IV only.
   d. I, II, III, and IV.

64. A matrix organization would be most appropriate for a:
   a. Company operating a set of geographically dispersed telephone call centers that provide technical support.
   b. Company that starts several complex, multidisciplinary engineering and construction projects each year.
   c. Retail company that sells to customers through multiple stores, located in shopping malls, as well as through a Web site and mailed catalogs.
   d. Company that provides temporary staffing to a wide variety of commercial and governmental agencies.

65. Which of the following is **not** an advantage of decentralization?
   a. Decisions are more easily made.
   b. Motivation of managers increases.
   c. Greater uniformity in decisions is achieved.
   d. Problems can be resolved immediately.

66. A network organizational structure is one in which:
   a. An employee reports to two supervisors.
   b. Authority and responsibility are concentrated at the top of the organization.
   c. Labor is specialized.
   d. Major business functions are subcontracted to third-party providers.

67. Departmentalization may be performed by:

   I. Function.
   II. Product.
   III. Geography.

   a. I only.
   b. II only.
   c. I and II only.
   d. I, II, and III.

68. Which of the following can be a limiting factor associated with group decision making?
   a. Groups generally do not analyze problems in enough depth.
   b. It is very difficult to get individuals to accept decisions made by groups.
   c. Groups have a difficult time identifying the important components of decision making.
   d. Accountability is dispersed when groups make decisions.

69. In which of the following situations would organizational politics most likely have a significant impact?
   a. When space allocations are made according to objective criteria.
   b. When the budget allows for generous salary increases for all employees.
   c. When promotions are based on an employee's attitude.
   d. When performance outcomes are clearly stated and objective.

70. Which of the following is true regarding groupthink?
   a. There is a tendency to conform to the majority's will and to ignore relevant individual input that is at variance with group opinion.
   b. The group is not required to reach consensus.
   c. The extent of groupthink is proportional to the size of the group.
   d. There are too many alternatives generated to facilitate decision making.

71. A project coordinator for a large capital project used a brainstorming session of the senior project managers to decide how to get the project back on schedule. A **disadvantage** of this approach is that:
   a. Responsibility for the decision will be unclear.
   b. Only situational factors will be addressed.
   c. Creativity will be decreased.
   d. Diversity of views will be decreased.

72. A team member who focuses on the overall perspective and reminds others of the vision, mission, or goal of the team informally assumes the role of a:
   a. Contributor.
   b. Collaborator.
   c. Communicator.
   d. Challenger.

73. Following a decision to change the composition of several work teams, management encounters significant resistance to the change from members of the teams. The most likely reason for the resistance is:
    a. Possible inefficiencies of the new arrangement.
    b. The breakup of existing teams.
    c. Understaffing for the tasks involved.
    d. The selection of a more costly approach to performing the assigned tasks.

74. Teams may be built by all the following methods **except**:
    a. Participating in a series of outdoor challenges.
    b. Incorporating a number of interdependent roles.
    c. Rating group effectiveness.
    d. Exerting direct pressure on dissenters.

75. When compared to individuals, groups have advantages and disadvantages for decision making. Which of the following is true regarding group decisions?

	Advantage	Disadvantage
a.	Increased personal accountability	Disagreements do not surface because of pressures to conform
b.	Increased acceptance of a decision by participants	More time needed to arrive at a decision
c.	Less time needed to arrive at a decision	Lack of personal accountability
d.	Increased diversity of expertise	Reduced acceptance of decision by participants

76. Which of the following is vital to maintaining team empowerment?
    a. Provide structure to team members.
    b. Monitor progress and offer timely feedback on performance.
    c. Reduce authority of the team when mistakes are made.
    d. Avoid tension and conflict within the team.

77. Which of the following is **not** an appropriate approach to team building?
    a. Ensuring a balance of complementary team roles.
    b. Choosing members based on their need to improve their skills.
    c. Developing clear and shared values.
    d. Selecting team members based on how they are likely to relate to each other.

78. Which of the following indicates a high-performance team?
    a. Pride in the team leader.
    b. Quick agreement on the first proposed solution for problems facing the team.
    c. Cautiousness in risk-taking.
    d. Commitment to personal growth of team members.

79. Which of the following is an indicator of interpersonal skills that are necessary for members of a team?
    I. Routinely keeps superiors, team members, and other appropriate parties informed of significant developments.
    II. Spends sufficient time cultivating contacts with peers to obtain timely information or resolve issues outside formal channels.
    III. Routinely assumes an appropriate amount of work or responsibility for group projects.

    a. I only.
    b. I and II only.
    c. II and III only.
    d. I, II, and III.

80. Which of the following scenarios illustrates an organization that has become out of balance by focusing too much on efficiency rather than effectiveness?
    a. The job is not completed and resources are wasted.
    b. The job is completed but resources are wasted.
    c. The job is not completed but resources are not wasted.
    d. The job is completed and resources are not wasted.

81. Which of the following is **not** an effective principle for guiding a manager's use of leadership techniques?
    a. Serve as a model of the behaviour expected from others.
    b. Value accountability.
    c. Value differences.
    d. Follow written procedures at all times.

82. A production team has worked well together for several years. However, severe arguments have recently occurred between two members of the team, and other members have begun to take sides, causing a negative effect on production performance. The best leadership style for the manager in this situation is:
    a. Directive.
    b. Supportive.
    c. Participative.
    d. Achievement-oriented.

83. A manager in a government agency supervises a section of clerical employees who review license applications for approval or denial. The clerical jobs are well-defined procedurally and are subject to government regulations. In this situation, what is the best leadership style for the manager?
    a. Directive.
    b. Supportive.
    c. Participative.
    d. Achievement-oriented.

84. The belief that successful leadership occurs when the leader's style matches the situation is the basis for:
    a. The contingency approach to leadership.
    b. The managerial-grid model of leadership.
    c. A behavioral approach to leadership.
    d. An achievement-oriented approach to leadership theories.

85. An employee is technically outstanding and works well with customers, but is not good at leading a team. To improve the employee's performance, the employee should be:
    a. Put in charge of the biggest project; the only way to learn is by performing the task.
    b. Put in charge of small projects with set milestones and a fully trained staff.
    c. Sent to school for management theory classes.
    d. Left alone and given assignments that accentuate personal strengths and avoid personal weaknesses.

86. Which of the following traits is the most important in order to succeed as a project manager?
    a. Budgeting and accounting knowledge.
    b. People management skills, such as conflict resolution and negotiation.
    c. Statistical analysis and process design experience.
    d. Strategic management tools and training.

87. A leader who explains decisions and provides opportunity for clarification is described as having which type of leadership style?
    a. Selling.
    b. Telling.
    c. Participating.
    d. Delegating.

88. An internal audit department adopts a training posture that provides training to management on fraud awareness, including an overview of the corporate fraud policy and hotline. This training posture best demonstrates that the internal audit department is taking which of the following leadership roles?
    a. Pathfinding, which focuses on "What is our purpose and how will we achieve it?"
    b. Aligning, which focuses on "How do we align systems and processes to achieve our purpose?"
    c. Empowering, which focuses on "How do we cultivate our people to have the right authority, responsibility, and commitment to help us best achieve our purpose?"
    d. Modeling, which focuses on "How do we demonstrate the values to convince others to follow us and take responsibility for achieving our purpose?"

89. Which of the following are conditions for a successful mentoring relationship?
    I. The relationship should be aimed at improvement of the mentee.
    II. The relationship should be based on growth of the mentee.
    III. The pairing of mentor and mentee should be voluntary.
    IV. Mentoring requires a positive work environment.

    a. I and II only.
    b. III and IV only.
    c. I, II, and III only.
    d. I, II, III, and IV.

90. Which of the following is the leadership style in which the leader and the followers make decisions on the basis of consensus?
    a. Autocratic.
    b. Benevolent authoritative.
    c. Consultative.
    d. Participative.

91. Which of the following conflict resolution techniques has the goal of maintaining harmonious relationships by placing another's needs and concerns above one's own?
    a. Accommodation.
    b. Compromise.
    c. Collaboration.
    d. Avoidance.

92. When performing a successful negotiation, a negotiator should:
    a. Understand the implications for both sides if the negotiation fails.
    b. Concentrate solely on the issues in the negotiation.
    c. Not deviate from stated positions.
    d. Depend on the initial research prepared for the negotiation.

93. What is a primary **disadvantage** of forcing another party to accept terms in a negotiation?
    a. Damage of the relationship between the negotiators.
    b. Lack of achievement of the negotiator's goals.
    c. Increased time involved in reaching an agreement.
    d. Reduction in internal support for the negotiator's tactics.

94. When negotiating with an analytical personality, the negotiator should:
    a. Present facts and precedents in an organized manner.
    b. Push the other party for quick closure of negotiations.
    c. Focus on creating a bond with the other party.
    d. Include unimportant items in the proposal for bargaining.

95. While negotiating a contract with a supplier's representative, a manager encounters unexpected resistance. The manager should first:
    a. Attempt to determine the reason behind the resistance.
    b. Stop the meeting and address the representative's concerns privately.
    c. Restate the manager's position regarding the issue.
    d. Determine the representative's views and requirements by researching the supplier.

96. Conflict arising as a result of a sales manager making delivery promises to customers that are incompatible with the low inventory levels maintained by the production manager is an example of which of the following types of interpersonal conflict?
    a. Personal differences.
    b. Information deficiency.
    c. Role incompatibility.
    d. Environmental stress.

97. Which of the following statements regarding approaches to conflict resolution is correct?
    a. Forcing is a style of managing conflict where the relationship is given more importance than individual goals, and goals are conceded in order to preserve relationships.
    b. Withdrawing is a style of managing conflict where personal goals and relationships are relinquished. It is regarded as a temporary solution because the problem and conflict continue to reoccur.
    c. Smoothing occurs when goals are highly important while the relationship is of minor importance. Goals are achieved at any cost.
    d. Compromising highly values goals and relationships. Conflicts are viewed as problems to be solved, and negotiators seek a solution that both achieves goals and improves relationships.

98. Keeping a conflict from surfacing at all is an example of following which conflict management strategy?
    a. Avoidance.
    b. Defusion.
    c. Containment.
    d. Confrontation.

99. Added-value negotiation is characterized by:
    a. One party approaching another with a proposal.
    b. A series of offers and counteroffers between the negotiating parties.
    c. One party approaching another with several proposals.
    d. One party quickly conceding to the demands of the other.

100. The method of principled negotiation is based on which of the following principles?

  I. Separate the people from the problem.
  II. Focus on positions, not interests.
  III. Invent options for mutual gain.
  IV. Insist on using subjective criteria.

  a. I and II only.
  b. I and III only.
  c. I, II, and III only.
  d. II, III, and IV only.

END OF PART IV QUESTIONS

PLEASE NOTE: The actual CIA exam Part IV will contain **125 exam questions**. The 125 questions will include up to 25 unscored questions, which will be used for research purposes. These unscored questions will be interspersed with the scored questions and will not be identified as unscored questions. Candidates should therefore answer all 125 questions to the best of their ability.

Solutions for Part IV – Business Management Skills

The solutions and suggested explanations for Part IV of the Certified Internal Auditor Model Exam Questions are provided on the following pages.

The chart below cross-references the question numbers for Part IV with the topics tested:

Topic Tested	Question Number
Strategic Management	1 – 28
Global Business Environments	29 – 43
Organizational Behavior	44 – 67
Management Skills	68 – 90
Negotiating	91 – 100

1. **Solution: c**
   a. Incorrect. Misleading other firms into taking or not taking an action to benefit the firm is a bluff. Bluff is a form of market signal that is not intended to be carried out.
   b. Incorrect. Market signal by a competitor that provides a direct or indirect indication of its intentions, motives, goals, or internal situation, is an indirect means of communicating in the market place and an essential input in competitor analysis.
   c. Correct. Initiating a move in the market where the competitor is strong is a cross-parry. Cross-parry is an effective way to indirectly signal displeasure and raise the threat of more serious retribution.
   d. Incorrect. Direct aggressive moves are aimed at reducing the performance of significant competitors or threaten their goals and is likely to cause a counter move.

2. **Solution: d**
   a. Incorrect. The role of strategic apex through direct supervision is limited, due to standardized skills in a professional bureaucracy.
   b. Incorrect. Technostructure's role of setting rules and procedures is limited, due to standardized skills in a professional bureaucracy.
   c. Incorrect. Line management's role of administering is limited, due to standardized skills in a professional bureaucracy.
   d. Correct. The operating core is the key in a professional bureaucracy because of the emphasis on standardized skills. Professional bureaucracy engages people with standardized skill sets and allows them to function in an unsupervised manner.

3. **Solution: b**
   a. Incorrect. Cost leadership is being the lowest-cost producer in the industry as whole.
   b. Correct. A cost focus strategy aims to be a cost leader for a particular market segment.
   c. Incorrect. Cost differentiation aims at providing a product at different costs in different market segments.
   d. Incorrect. Cost containment aims at controlling costs related to a particular product or market.

4. **Solution: a**
   a. Correct. The impact of Porter's five forces determines the competency intensity and the potential profitability of the industry, where the profitability is measured in terms of long-term return on capital invested.
   b. Incorrect. The entrance barrier is one of the five forces that should be measured to define the competency intensity and the potential profitability.
   c. Incorrect. Rivalry is one of the five forces that should be measured to define the competency intensity and the potential profitability.
   d. Incorrect. The analysis of the five forces is only one step in the definition of the strategy.

5. **Solution: b**
   a. Incorrect. This is a product-oriented definition.
   b. Correct. This is a market-oriented definition as opposed to the product-oriented definition of "we sell gasoline."
   c. Incorrect. This is a product-oriented definition.
   d. Incorrect. This is a product-oriented definition.

6. **Solution: b**
   a. Incorrect. Technology transfer constitutes technology synergy.
   b. Correct. Bundling of products, distribution through the same distribution channels, or usage of the same sales force are examples for market synergies.
   c. Incorrect. The production of multiple products at one production facility is an example of cost synergy.
   d. Incorrect. Using complementary management skills is an example of management synergy.

7. **Solution: c (I, II, and III only)**
   I, II, III. Correct. These strategies will challenge the organization to upgrade and improve and will also reward employees for innovation.
   IV. Incorrect. A focus only on performance outcomes will discourage employees from taking risks and hence hinder innovation.

8. **Solution: b (I and II only)**
   I, II. Correct. These are two of the five basic forces that drive industry competition. The others are bargaining power of buyers, threat of substitution, and rivalry among current competitors.
   III. Incorrect. Labor unrest and material shortages are short-run factors that affect access to raw materials and may therefore affect competition and profitability, but these are not among the five basic forces driving competition.
   IV. Incorrect. This is one of the six major sources of barriers to entry. The others are economies of scale, capital requirements, switching costs, access to distribution channels, and government policy.

9. **Solution: c**
   a. Incorrect. Consolidation is characteristic of a mature industry environment.
   b. Incorrect. Competitive interdependence is characteristic of a mature industry environment.
   c. Correct. Falling demand is characteristic of declining industries.
   d. Incorrect. Strategic focus on deterring entry of new competitors into the marketplace is characteristic of a mature industry environment.

10. **Solution: c**
    a. Incorrect. See answer "c".
    b. Incorrect. See answer "c".
    c. Correct. Strategies such as chaining, franchising, and horizontal mergers are commonly used in fragmented industries, because there are low barriers to entry. Companies in fragmented industries face many opportunities for differentiation but each opportunity for competitive advantage is small.
    d. Incorrect. See answer "c".

11. **Solution: d (I, II, III, and IV)**
    I, II, III, IV. Correct. Costs that management should consider would include costs of retraining employees; costs of acquiring new ancillary equipment; write-offs of undepreciated investments in the old technology; capital requirements and research and development costs of the changeover; and costs of modifying interrelated stages of production or related aspects of the business.

12. **Solution: b**
    a. Incorrect. Low fixed costs generally imply weak barriers to entry and consequent ability of local competitors to effectively engage against a larger global firm.
    b. Correct. To the extent that production of each unit is cheaper than the last, this favors large concentrated producers on a global scale. (The archetypal example is oil refining.)
    c. Incorrect. Weak copyright protection or intellectual property rights enforcement would enable small local competitors to produce efficiently, if illicitly, in the short term.
    d. Incorrect. To the extent that a product requires local service, this dilutes the advantage of being a large and efficient global competitor.

13. **Solution: c (I, II, and III only)**
    I, II, III. Correct. The government normally restricts trade in order to foster national security, develop new industries, and protect declining industries.
    IV. Incorrect. Increasing tax revenues would not be an impetus for governments to restrict trade, because tax revenues would decrease with lessened trade.

14. **Solution: a**
    a. Correct. This is a social trend.
    b. Incorrect. This is a political trend where the government is involved.
    c. Incorrect. Inflation is connected with the economy; hence, this is an economic trend.
    d. Incorrect. This represents a technological trend.

15. **Solution: a**
    a. Correct. The subsidies for new players weaken the entrance barriers of the industry, allowing new players to get into the industry and producing a higher rivalry among more competitors.
    b. Incorrect. The differentiation of products is considered an entrance barrier that discourages potential new players to get into the industry (because they are incapable of offering a comparable product) while protecting the industry's profitability.
    c. Incorrect. The learning period of the industry is an asset that new players must acquire. This cost in some cases becomes extremely high and may discourage new players from entering the industry.
    d. Incorrect. Low exit fixed costs produce an easy exit players when they decide to leave the industry, but exit costs would not particularly encourage entry of new players.

16. **Solution: b**
    a. Incorrect. There is no need of backward integration if the firm's current suppliers are highly reliable.
    b. Correct. Backward integration is appropriate when the firm's current suppliers are unreliable.
    c. Incorrect. Backward integration is a form of vertical integration that involves the purchase of suppliers in order to reduce dependency. The location of the suppliers is not an issue.
    d. Incorrect. See answer "c".

17. **Solution: b**
    a. Incorrect. Just-in-time (JIT) production can increase dependency on suppliers.
    b. Correct. JIT production can reduce the cost of implementing new strategies.
    c. Incorrect. JIT production will increase the flexibility of production facilities.
    d. Incorrect. JIT production would not affect the need to for a dependable workforce.

18. **Solution: c**
    a. Incorrect. Developing products involves adding more value or features to the existing product. The opportunity for franchising is based on standardization of products.
    b. Incorrect. Differentiating products implies that the products are to be different in different markets. This is not generally the basis for franchising.
    c. Correct. Standardizing products means to maintain the same product or standardize the production, operations, and facilities in different locations or markets. This standardization provides the opportunity for franchising.
    d. Incorrect. Diversifying products means to deal in different, either related or unrelated, products. Franchising is usually based on standardization, rather than differentiation, of products.

19. **Solution: a**
    a. Correct. Market penetration is growth of existing products and/or development of existing markets.
    b. Incorrect. Market development seeks new markets for current products.
    c. Incorrect. Product development involves launching new products to existing markets.
    d. Incorrect. Diversification is launching new products for new markets.

20. **Solution: b**
    a. Incorrect. Horizontal integration may be described as adding new products to existing markets or new markets to existing products.
    b. Correct. Vertical integration occurs when a company becomes its own supplier or distributor.
    c. Incorrect. Concentric diversification occurs when a company adds new products which have technological synergies with the existing products.
    d. Incorrect. Conglomerate diversification means making new products for an entirely new class of customers.

21. **Solution: d (I, II, and IV only)**
    I, II, IV. Correct. A firm may adopt a build strategy for this type of strategic business unit (SBU) if the SBU shows a strong potential to grow, if the firm is willing to forego short-term earnings and cash flow, and if the firm is willing and has the capacity to finance its growth.
    III. Incorrect. A firm that expects a short-term increase in cash flow may adopt either a divest or a harvest strategy but not a build strategy because this type of SBU needs a lot of cash flow to finance its growth.

22. **Solution: d**
    a. Incorrect. Objectives are vital to target setting and establishing a sense of direction, without which unnecessary time and cost are incurred.
    b. Incorrect. Objective setting very often involves negotiation.
    c. Incorrect. Objectives are more precise statements of direction.
    d. Correct. Objectives need to be continually updated to reflect the environmental changes.

23. **Solution: d**
    a. Incorrect. A cash cow generates more cash than it requires, providing funds to the corporation to invest in other ventures.
    b. Incorrect. Question marks deserve attention to determine if the venture is viable or not. The business is located in a growing industry but has not achieved a strong competitive position.
    c. Incorrect. Dogs describe a business situated in a low growth or declining industry and if not positioned strongly will be divested.
    d. Correct. Stars describe a business with a strong competitive position in the industry. The industry is robust and SBUs are highly attractive. Net cash flow is modest since investment is heavy although stars generate large amounts of cash.

24. **Solution: b**
    a. Incorrect. Decline in inventory levels is not the first symptom of the decline stage as it will occur only when production need will decline as a result of decline in sales. Also, a decline in inventory levels could be a result of a change to just-in-time production.
    b. Correct. The sales of most product forms and brands eventually drop. The decline may be slow or rapid. This is the first symptom of the decline stage.
    c. Incorrect. Decline in production may be due to plant technological reasons or due to unavailability of raw materials in any stage of the product life cycle.
    d. Incorrect. Alteration in prices is a marketing decision. This action may be taken in the maturity stage in order to compete in the market. It is not a symptom of the decline stage.

25. **Solution: b**
    a. Incorrect. This is the case during the introduction stage of the product life cycle.
    b. Correct. During growth stage of the product life cycle, product reliability becomes more important.
    c. Incorrect. This is the case during the maturity stage of the product life cycle.
    d. Incorrect. This is the case during the decline stage of the product life cycle.

26. Solution: a
a. Correct. At the introduction stage, expensive sales promotion needs to be undertaken in order to educate the consumer and develop market acceptance.
b. Incorrect. At the introduction stage, competitors do not tend to enter in the product market.
c. Incorrect. At the introduction stage, overproduction is unlikely and would not affect sales growth.
d. Incorrect. At the introduction stage, not many alternatives are available.

27. Solution: c
a. Incorrect. During the introduction stage, there is little or no competition, so prices are at their highest. Also, costs are high in the introduction stage.
b. Incorrect. During the growth stage, prices will be lower than during the introduction stage, but not as low as during the maturity stage. Costs are dropping and competitors are being added, but costs are not at their minimum and competitors are not at their maximum
c. Correct. During the maturity stage, competition is at its greatest, and costs are at their lowest; thus, prices would be at their lowest.
d. Incorrect. During the decline stage, there are few competitors, so prices can be raised. In addition, costs are on the rise because volume is declining.

28. Solution: b
a. Incorrect. Costs are high during the introduction stage, and volume is low.
b. Correct. During the growth stage, the opportunity for cost reductions is at its maximum because volume is increased at a high rate; thus, fixed costs are being spread over more units of production and the benefits of the learning curve are being realized.
c. Incorrect. Since volume is not changing much during the maturity stage, there is less opportunity for cost reductions.
d. Incorrect. Costs per unit typically rise during the decline stage because volume declines. Also, cost increases can more easily be passed along to customers because there are few competitors.

29. Solution: b
a. Incorrect. Because an increased sales price would raise corporate profits, the tax revenue lost through eliminating cartel activity would serve as a disincentive to government anti-cartel efforts.
b. Correct. Governments and international organizations seek to protect consumers and the health of the domestic and global economy through anti-cartel efforts.
c. Incorrect. Although the effect of cartel activities may be harmful to small businesses, the greatest impact is on the overall economy.
d. Incorrect. While a free market may contribute to the stability of developing countries' economies, this does not provide a compelling reason for domestic anti-cartel efforts in industrialized countries.

30. Solution: b
a. Incorrect. This is the definition of grey markets.
b. Correct. This is the definition of dumping.
c. Incorrect. See answer "b".
d. Incorrect. See answer "b".

31. Solution: a
a. Correct. Personal mastery or self-control is a personal dimension rather than a cultural one.
b. Incorrect. Power distance is a cultural dimension referring to the extent to which power is distributed unequally among individuals.
c. Incorrect. Masculinity versus femininity is a cultural dimension referring to the dominance of assertiveness and acquisition of things (labeled masculine) versus concern for people, feelings, and the quality of life (labeled feminine).
d. Incorrect. The extent to which one feels threatened by ambiguous situations and avoids conflict is a cultural dimension called uncertainty avoidance.

32. **Solution: b (I and III only)**
    I. Correct. By encouraging groups to identify novel or unusual contributions, brainstorming helps make all of the elements of a problem and its resolution visible.
    II. Incorrect. By identifying views without further analysis, polling does not increase understanding of a complex situation.
    III. Correct. Lateral thinking explores different ways of looking at an issue, thereby increasing the likelihood of finding better solutions.

33. **Solution: c**
    a. Incorrect. Response time is not a significant issue.
    b. Incorrect. Taxation is not the most significant issue.
    c. Correct. Country-specific privacy laws can be very stringent about customer data crossing borders.
    d. Incorrect. Backup and recovery are not significant impediments.

34. **Solution: c**
    a. Incorrect. These are the driving forces for localization, not globalization.
    b. Incorrect. These are the three benefits of localization.
    c. Correct. These factors favor globalization by reducing trade barriers, reducing cost of co-ordination, increasing economies of scale, and encouraging standardization and global branding.
    d. Incorrect. These are the determinants of a global business strategy.

35. **Solution: b**
    a. Incorrect. Ethnocentrism is characterized by a home-country orientation. The company focuses on its domestic market and sees exports as secondary.
    b. Correct. The company adapts itself to the local environment under a polycentric orientation. Examples include various subsidiaries of a multinational corporation.
    c. Incorrect. Geocentrism is based on the assumption that similarities in the world can be incorporated to form a global strategy.
    d. Incorrect. Regiocentrism is based on the assumption that similarities in the region can be incorporated into business objectives or strategies.

36. **Solution: a**
    a. Correct. Cost benefits are obtained from economies of scale owing to standardization of products and/or processes, as well as increased bargaining power over suppliers of raw materials, components, and services.
    b. Incorrect. Timing benefits are obtained due to coordinated approaches in product launching in the early stages of the product life cycle.
    c. Incorrect. Learning benefits accrue from the coordinated transfer of information, best practices, and people across subsidiaries.
    d. Incorrect. Arbitrage benefits accrue from the advantages that a global company can gain by using resources in one country for the benefit of a subsidiary in another country.

37. **Solution: a**
    a. Correct. Attitudes, tastes, behavior, and social codes are the components of the cultural factors. This is therefore an instance of a cultural factor.
    b. Incorrect. Distribution, customization, and responsiveness comprise the commercial factors.
    c. Incorrect. Standards, spatial presence, transportation, and languages constitute the technical factors.
    d. Incorrect. Regulation and national security issues constitute the legal factors.

38. Solution: b
   a. Incorrect. Declaring lower profits in countries with lower taxation will not achieve the tax objective.
   b. Correct. Declaring higher profits in countries with lower tax levels will reduce tax liability.
   c. Incorrect. Charging higher prices will reduce both income and tax liability, which is not the optimum situation.
   d. Incorrect. Lower prices will cause higher earnings and higher tax liability.

39. Solution: c
   a. Incorrect. Perceptual problems stem from differences in each person's interpretation of reality.
   b. Incorrect. Stereotyping is a tendency to perceive another person as belonging to a particular or single class or category.
   c. Correct. Ethnocentrism leads people to believe that they are best in every thing regardless of the topic under discussion. This spirit is promoted through the value structures and nationalistic spirit of the people.
   d. Incorrect. Uncertainty avoidance refers to the extent to which people feel threatened by ambiguous situations and the degree to which they try to avoid these situations.

40. Solution: b
   a. Incorrect. Economic risk is the likelihood that economic mismanagement will cause changes in the country's business environment that will hurt the profit and other goals of the company.
   b. Correct. Political risk is the likelihood that political forces will cause changes in the country's business environment that will hurt the profit and other goals of the company. Nationalism, expropriation, and terrorism are all examples of political risk.
   c. Incorrect. Operational risk is uncertainty of non-financial events that may result in failure of the organization and related financial losses.
   d. Incorrect. Environmental risk is the uncertainly and severity of the impact of potential environmental hazards.

41. Solution: d (II, III, IV, and V only)
   I. Incorrect. Communication difficulties due to long distances separating senders and receivers have been minimized by electronic communication such as electronic mail, fax, and teleconferencing.
   II. Correct. Body language and other forms of non-verbal communication may have different meanings in different cultures.
   III. Correct. Language is frequently a cause of miscommunication because all parties may not have mastery of the language.
   IV. Correct. Attitudes, such as stereotypes, may cause misunderstandings.
   V. Correct. Time is a barrier to international communication because different cultures regard and use time differently.

42. Solution: c
   a. Incorrect. When global forces dominate, local adaptation and responsiveness are ignored.
   b. Incorrect. When local forces dominate, efficiency, speed, arbitrage, and learning are ignored.
   c. Correct. Competitiveness cannot be achieved without achieving the benefits of global Integration and coordination as well as the benefits of localization, which include flexibility, proximity, and quick response time.
   d. Incorrect. When neither of the forces dominates, a competitive positioning cannot at all be attained.

43. Solution: b
    a. Incorrect. This is a key disadvantage of a geocentric staffing policy, not an ethnocentric policy. Although relocation costs and higher compensation are required for expatriate managers in the ethnocentric strategy, it allows overall compensation structure to follow the national levels in each country, reducing the overall staffing costs.
    b. Correct. This is the key disadvantage of an ethnocentric staffing policy.
    c. Incorrect. An ethnocentric staffing policy strategy limits career mobility of host-country employees, not parent-company employees.
    d. Incorrect. This is a disadvantage of a polycentric staffing policy.

44. Solution: d
    a. Incorrect. Autonomous work teams are only one type of job enrichment and are not applicable in many situations.
    b. Incorrect. While enlarging jobs to add different tasks may be a motivating factor, adding more similar tasks does not fundamentally redesign jobs and may be demotivating if existing tasks are difficult or boring.
    c. Incorrect. Rotation does not fundamentally redesign jobs.
    d. Correct. One of the major principles of successful job design and redesign is to take into account employee needs and skills and match them with jobs, or change their jobs to fit those needs and skills.

45. Solution: b
    a. Incorrect. Attractive pension provisions would meet an employee's physiological needs.
    b. Correct. Challenging new job assignments would meet an employee's self-actualization needs.
    c. Incorrect. Good working conditions would meet an employee's physiological needs.
    d. Incorrect. Regular positive feedback would meet an employee's esteem needs.

46. Solution: c
    a. Incorrect. The equity theory focuses on the balance between inputs and outcomes.
    b. Incorrect. The basis of the expectancy theory is that employees are only motivated to provide inputs if they believe a given level of outcome will result.
    c. Correct. The need theory suggests that employees have needs that they are motivated to satisfy in the workplace.
    d. Incorrect. The goal-setting theory is based upon the belief that employees have desires and aspirations, which result in goals that direct their behavior.

47. Solution: c
    a. Incorrect. Job enlargement is a horizontal extension of the job, in order to span a larger part of the total production work.
    b. Incorrect. Job enrichment is a vertical extension of the job, in order to build greater responsibility, breadth of work, and challenge into a job.
    c. Correct. The absence of job security would lead to dissatisfaction but its presence would not lead to superior performance or job satisfaction.
    d. Incorrect. Job rotation would result in greater satisfaction because the employee has a greater understanding of the work process.

48. Solution: b
    a. Incorrect. Positive reinforcement strengthens and increases behavior by the presentation of a desirable consequence.
    b. Correct. Negative reinforcement strengthens the response and increases the probability of repetition of avoiding undesirable consequences of any action.
    c. Incorrect. A reward is simply something that the person who presents it deems to be desirable.
    d. Incorrect. Negative reinforcement strengthens and increases behavior while punishment weakens and decreases behavior.

49. **Solution: b**
    a. Incorrect. Social rewards normally include acknowledgement of employee achievement through actions such as solicitation of advice.
    b. Correct. These are normally non-recurring awards, showing appreciation for the role of the employee; other similar examples are gift coupons, stock options, early time off with pay, or dinner and theater tickets.
    c. Incorrect. Examples of visual or auditory awards include a private office, book-club discussions, or redecoration of the work environment.
    d. Incorrect. Examples of manipulatables are gifts, such as desk accessories, watches, trophies, clothing, or rings.

50. **Solution: b**
    a. Incorrect. Job enlargement involves expanding a job horizontally.
    b. Correct. When work is becoming too routine, such training keeps staff from becoming bored.
    c. Incorrect. Job enrichment involves the vertical expansion of a job, to allow the worker to control planning, execution, and work evaluation.
    d. Incorrect. Job variety is not a work redesign option but rather a function of the job.

51. **Solution: d (I, II, and III)**
    I. Correct. Performance feedback is an important part of goal-based approaches to motivating employees.
    II. Correct. Presenting opportunities for responsibilities will motivate employees by helping them meet the need for achievement.
    III. Correct. Satisfying personal needs is a method of motivating employees.

52. **Solution: a**
    a. Correct. Filtering involves the sender of a message manipulating information so that it will be seen more favorably by the receiver.
    b. Incorrect. Selective perception involves the receivers selectively interpreting what they see or hear based on their interests, background, experience, and attitudes.
    c. Incorrect. Emotions affect the interpretation of the message, not the contents.
    d. Incorrect. Choice of language involves the personal selection of words to communicate the same message without distorting it.

53. **Solution: c (I, II, and IV only)**
    I. Correct. Summarizing brings the discussion into focus and clarifies priorities.
    II. Correct. Clarifying content or process helps others explore the problem and make their ideas more concrete.
    III. Incorrect. Evaluating may curtail the presentation of views and lead another person to believe that the listener's mind is already made up.
    IV. Correct. Empathizing shows that the listener understands how the other person feels and encourages them to express their feelings.

54. **Solution: d**
    a. Incorrect. Listening for emotions enables the detection of strong emotions inhibiting rational problem resolution and the likelihood of consensus.
    b. Incorrect. Asking thoughtful questions shows that one is listening deeply and encourages people to arrive at their own solutions.
    c. Incorrect. Listening to how a person is solving the problem allows the provision of comments on process as well as content.
    d. Correct. By interrupting the speaker, even with good intentions, the listener may inhibit further communication and may be jumping to unwarranted conclusions.

55. Solution: b
a. Incorrect. See answer "b".
b. Correct. They are examples of downward communication.
c. Incorrect. See answer "b".
d. Incorrect. See answer "b".

56. Solution: a (I and II only)
I. Correct. Information overload and misrepresentation of feelings and emotions are considered drawbacks of electronic communication. Information overload, such as numerous electronic mail messages, may lead to lost time and inefficiencies, and is considered a drawback of electronic communication.
II. Correct. Electronic mail cannot accurately convey the feeling and tone intended by the person initiating the communication and may be misinterpreted by the receiver. This is considered a drawback of electronic communication.
III. Incorrect. Reduced transmission time is considered a positive result of electronic communication.
IV. Incorrect. Electronic communication generally results in an adequate paper trail (such as saved "sent mail").

57. Solution: b
a. Incorrect. This is not the best measure to use. For example, a department that sells books may serve a lot of customers or sell many units, but that does not mean that it is more productive than a department that sells furniture.
b. Correct. A critical output of interest is revenue per square foot. The floor space in the store is a limited resource whose productivity should be analyzed.
c. Incorrect. See answer "a".
d. Incorrect. The number of items stocked in a given department says nothing about productivity.

58. Solution: d
a. Incorrect. This response illustrates two of the characteristics of organizational decline: increased centralization of decision making and lack of long-term planning. The exclusive emphasis on short-term results is likely to be counterproductive.
b. Incorrect. Another characteristic of organizational decline is nonprioritized cuts. Downsizing, by itself, rarely turns a company around.
c. Incorrect. This is too crude a method of prioritizing cuts. Reducing staff disproportionately in control functions could have disastrous consequences.
d. Correct. This is a long-term solution which contains the elements needed to counter organizational decline.

59. Solution: c
a. Incorrect. This is not an efficiency measure because there is not any comparison of input to output.
b. Incorrect. This is an example of effectiveness, not efficiency.
c. Correct. Efficiency is the ratio of effective output to the input required to achieve it. Insurance claims processed per day measures the output (claims processed) to the input (a day's work).
d. Incorrect. This is not an efficiency measure because there is not any comparison of input to output.

60. Solution: d (I, II, III, and IV)
I, II, III, IV. Correct. All are required to align managerial goals with organizational goals.

61. Solution: b
   a. Incorrect. Narrow spans of control are typically found in tall organizations with many more levels.
   b. Correct. Narrow spans of control mean that the ratio of those supervised (subordinates) to those performing the supervision (managers) is lower.
   c. Incorrect. Narrow spans of control result in higher administrative expense and less self-management.
   d. Incorrect. Wider spans of control allow subordinates more discretion.

62. Solution: b
   a. Incorrect. If substantial planning were required, a manager would benefit from reduced supervision requirements. Also, increased planning implies a changing environment, where work of subordinates will be changing over time, requiring significant managerial work for training.
   b. Correct. If substantial coordination were required, a manager would benefit from reduced supervision requirements. In addition, increased coordination implies that the work performed by subordinates is not standardized.
   c. Incorrect. Geographically dispersed subordinates would justify a narrow span of control.
   d. Incorrect. With very similar work, subordinates can train one another, provide backup if one subordinate is not present, and verify one another's work. In addition, work procedures are relatively easy to document and a manager can be knowledgeable about the work of everyone doing something similar.

63. Solution: d (I, II, III, and IV)
   I, II, III, IV. Correct. All are typical inputs for a 360-degree performance appraisal process.

64. Solution: b
   a. Incorrect. Individuals assigned to work in one call center would have only one supervisor, who would be located in that call center.
   b. Correct. A matrix organization that would assign specialists as needed to various projects would be appropriate for such a company.
   c. Incorrect. While multi-channel sales requires coordination, there is no reason to believe that staff would be moved from one sales channel to another for project work, or that they would report to two different supervisors.
   d. Incorrect. Temporary staff do not report to any manager within a temporary agency – they simply work for a wide variety of employers, who have full authority. They are not necessarily specialized staff, and if not needed, they are simply not paid.

65. Solution: c
   a. Incorrect. Ease of decision making is an advantage of decentralization.
   b. Incorrect. Increase in managers' motivation is an advantage of decentralization.
   c. Correct. Increased uniformity in decisions is an advantage of centralization.
   d. Incorrect. Immediacy of problem resolution is an advantage of decentralization.

66. Solution: d
   a. Incorrect. This is a distinguishing feature of a matrix structure.
   b. Incorrect. This is a characteristic of centralization.
   c. Incorrect. This is a characteristic of bureaucracy.
   d. Correct. The subcontracting of major business functions to others is a feature of network structures.

67. Solution: d (I, II, and III)
   I, II, III. Correct. Departmentalization may be performed by function, product, or geography.

68. Solution: d
 a. Incorrect. Groups may actually analyze problems in greater depth.
 b. Incorrect. Acceptance of decisions may actually be enhanced because participants usually view outcomes as "ours" rather than "theirs."
 c. Incorrect. Groups may actually do a better job of identifying important components.
 d. Correct. This is potentially a major problem associated with group decision making. When accountability is dispersed, it is often lost. That is why the group usually only provides advice and a particular person, such as an audit manager, makes the final decision, thus becoming accountable.

69. Solution: c
 a. Incorrect. Use of objective criteria minimizes the potential impact of organization politics.
 b. Incorrect. When all employees benefit, organizational politics would have less impact than if decisions were being made that benefited some employees and not others.
 c. Correct. Use of subjective criteria, such as attitude, rather than objective criteria, such as job performance, allows organizational politics to have a greater impact.
 d. Incorrect. See answer "a".

70. Solution: a
 a. Correct. Groupthink refers to the tendency to conform to the majority's will when there is individual input that is at variance with the group opinion. Groupthink is a concept that refers to faulty decision making in a group. Groups experiencing groupthink do not consider all alternatives, and they desire unanimity at the expense of quality decisions. Groupthink occurs when groups are highly cohesive and when they are under considerable pressure to make a quality decision.
 b. Incorrect. Consensus is desirable, even with groupthink.
 c. Incorrect. Groupthink is not limited to groups of only certain sizes, and the degree of groupthink is not in proportion to the group size.
 d. Incorrect. There are few or no alternatives addressed under groupthink.

71. Solution: a
 a. Correct. This is one of the major disadvantages of group decision making.
 b. Incorrect. This tendency does not depend on the fact that the problem is approached through group decision making.
 c. Incorrect. An advantage of group decision making through brainstorming is that creativity is increased.
 d. Incorrect. An advantage of group decision making through brainstorming is that it increases the diversity of views.

72. Solution: c
 a. Incorrect. A contributor is a task-oriented team member who provides the team with good technical information and data and pushes the team to set high-performance goals.
 b. Incorrect. A collaborator binds the whole team and is open and flexible to new ideas, willing to work outside the defined role, and willing to share the recognition and credit with other team members.
 c. Correct. A communicator is a people-oriented member, is process-driven, and is an effective listener who plays the role of a facilitator and a consensus builder.
 d. Incorrect. A challenger is candid and open, questions the team goals, is willing to disagree with the team leader, and encourages well-conceived risk taking.

73. **Solution: b**
    a. Incorrect. Complaints about "why it will not work" virtually always represent an "acceptable" roadblock to a plan that has unacceptable behavioral consequences.
    b. Correct. Members of cohesive work groups often exert pressure to resist changes that threaten to break up the group.
    c. Incorrect. Issues of under- or over-staffing for a task represent symptoms of resistance to change, but not the actual or root cause of the problem.
    d. Incorrect. Citing cost factors also represents an "acceptable" rationale to block the implementation of a new approach.

74. **Solution: d**
    a. Incorrect. This is a method of team building.
    b. Incorrect. This is a method of team building.
    c. Incorrect. This is a method of team building.
    d. Correct. This is a symptom of groupthink.

75. **Solution: b**
    a. Incorrect. Group decisions lead to a lack of personal accountability.
    b. Correct. An advantage of group decision making is that those who participated in a group process are more likely to accept and support the group's decisions. A disadvantage is that it takes more time to arrive at a decision in a group, compared to an individual making a decision.
    c. Incorrect. See answer "b".
    d. Incorrect. See answer "b".

76. **Solution: b**
    a. Incorrect. Team members seek structure at the beginning of team development, before empowerment.
    b. Correct. Monitoring and feedback are vital to maintaining the right level of empowerment.
    c. Incorrect. A tolerance for problems and mistakes is part of empowerment.
    d. Incorrect. Tension and conflict are a normal part of team development.

77. **Solution: b**
    a. Incorrect. Role definition is a recognized approach to team building.
    b. Correct. Skill development is not a recognized approach and should not be the driver in team building.
    c. Incorrect. Values development is a recognized approach to team building.
    d. Incorrect. Interpersonal relations is a recognized approach to team building.

78. **Solution: d**
    a. Incorrect. High-performance teams recognize the value of all members.
    b. Incorrect. This reflects a lack of diversity characteristic of groupthink.
    c. Incorrect. Individuals tend to be more risk-averse than as teams.
    d. Correct. This mutual support is characteristic of high-performance teams.

79. **Solution: b (I and II only)**
    I, II. Correct. Items I and II are elements of interpersonal skills that include interaction, cooperation, and ability to deal with people.
    III. Incorrect. Item III is an element of team participation.

80. **Solution: c**
    a. Incorrect. This scenario illustrates an organization out of balance by having no focus on either effectiveness or efficiency.
    b. Incorrect. This scenario illustrates an organization out of balance by focusing too much on effectiveness.
    c. Correct. This scenario illustrates an organization out of balance by focusing too much on efficiency.
    d. Incorrect. This scenario illustrates an organization perfectly balancing efficiency and effectiveness.

81. **Solution: d**
    a. Incorrect. Recursive leadership is important to gaining trust.
    b. Incorrect. This ensures high-value activities.
    c. Incorrect. Seeking synergies from diversity is an effective leadership habit.
    d. Correct. Focusing on internal process is a habit of administration and not of leadership.

82. **Solution: a**
    a. Correct. Directive leadership provides the highest subordinate satisfaction when a team encounters substantive internal conflict.
    b. Incorrect. Supportive style is best when tasks are highly structured, and there is a low level of stress and strife.
    c. Incorrect. Participative style is most useful when subordinates feel that they control their own destinies.
    d. Incorrect. Achievement-oriented style is optimal for situations in which tasks are ambiguously structured.

83. **Solution: b**
    a. Incorrect. Directive leadership provides the highest subordinate satisfaction when a team encounters substantive internal conflict.
    b. Correct. Supportive style is best when tasks are highly structured, and the authority relationships are clear and bureaucratic.
    c. Incorrect. Participative style is most useful when subordinates feel that they control their own destinies.
    d. Incorrect. Achievement-oriented style is optimal for situations in which tasks are ambiguously structured.

84. **Solution: a**
    a. Correct. The contingency approach is based on the principle that there is no one best way of leadership. According to that principle, the effective leadership style or behavior depends on the situation requirements. Therefore, the leader's style has to be matched to the situation either by changing the leader or changing the leader's behavior.
    b. Incorrect. The managerial-grid model is based on the assumption that the team management style is the most effective regardless of the situation. It therefore does not fit with the contingency view of leadership.
    c. Incorrect. The behavioral approach does not focus on the situation or the match between the leader and the situation. Instead the focus is on identification of leadership behaviors. The issue of contingent behaviors (matching behaviors to the situation) is not central to the behavioral approach.
    d. Incorrect. An achievement-oriented approach involves setting challenging goals and is not contingent on the situation

85. **Solution: b**
    a. Incorrect. The employee is unprepared for a major challenge. The employee will most likely fail, and feelings of failure discourage development.
    b. Correct. The size of the project, the firm guidance of milestones, and the strength of a fully trained staff will help the employee to succeed. Also, the staff will help to train the employee, who should learn some skills from this project and be ready for a slightly more challenging project.
    c. Incorrect. This could be somewhat helpful, but theory is less likely to develop the skills of leadership than experience in a good situation.
    d. Incorrect. This would avoid short-term problems but would not help the employee develop the skills needed to move ahead.

86. **Solution: b**
    a. Incorrect. Projects are ad hoc and temporary, and most challenges involve people and technical/technology issues.
    b. Correct. Projects are outside the normal organizational hierarchy or chain of command, so a project leader cannot rely on direct authority to accomplish what must be done by the various parts of an organization that are participating in a project.
    c. Incorrect. Statistical analysis and process design are skills that, if necessary in a project, would be employed by a subordinate, not the project manager.
    d. Incorrect. Strategic management is long-term, broad-based, and starts with relatively few constraints other than existing resources organization-wide, while project management is shorter-term and focused on a project that has been approved with specific resources.

87. **Solution: a**
    a. Correct. This is a description of a selling style of leadership.
    b. Incorrect. A telling leadership style provides specific instructions and closely supervises performance.
    c. Incorrect. A participating leadership style encourages the sharing of ideas and facilitates decision making.
    d. Incorrect. A delegating leadership style turns over responsibility for decisions and implementation.

88. **Solution: c**
    a. Incorrect. Pathfinding addresses establishment of purpose, mission, and/or vision.
    b. Incorrect. While fraud awareness could be deemed part of the alignment process, it is not the best answer because it is only one component of an overall fraud program.
    c. Correct. Empowering is the best answer because fraud awareness training as noted in the question provides individuals with the information and guidance that they need to take responsibility and commit to tasks required to achieve a purpose. Fraud awareness training makes sure that they know the policy and know how to report suspected issues.
    d. Incorrect. Training does not involve modeling the behavior.

89. **Solution: c (I, II, and III only)**
    I. Correct. Goals should include improved job performance and career potential.
    II. Correct. Growth, not creating dependency, is the desired outcome.
    III. Correct. Many mentoring programs failed when pairings were not voluntary.
    IV. Incorrect. Mentoring can be helpful in all work environments.

90. **Solution: d**
    a. Incorrect. Under the autocratic style, managers impose decisions on their subordinates.
    b. Incorrect. Under the benevolent authoritative style, the manager makes all the decisions but believes that the subordinates have to be motivated by rewards and that leadership is by a condescending form of the master-servant relationship.
    c. Incorrect. Under the consultative style, the manager confers with the subordinates and takes their views into account, makes the final decision.
    d. Correct. Under the participative style, the leader and followers make the decision on a democratic basis through consensus and the superiors have complete confidence in their subordinates.

91. **Solution: a**
    a. Correct. Accommodation is a resolution technique that has the goal of maintaining harmonious relationships.
    b. Incorrect. See answer "a".
    c. Incorrect. See answer "a".
    d. Incorrect. See answer "a".

92. **Solution: a**
    a. Correct. Negotiators should assess the best alternatives for both themselves and the other parties to determine their relative strength in the negotiation process. If alternatives are not readily available or are unattractive, a party is under additional pressure to make the negotiation work.
    b. Incorrect. Issues outside of the conflict itself may impact the negotiations.
    c. Incorrect. Flexibility may assist the negotiator in identifying alternatives.
    d. Incorrect. Additional research may be required to fully understand the other party's alternatives to negotiation.

93. **Solution: a**
    a. Correct. In future negotiations, the forced opponent will be less likely to work with the negotiator to achieve mutual goals. Negotiations in which one or both parties feels they must win at the expense of the other party ultimately do not build a relationship of trust and cooperation.
    b. Incorrect. The negotiator has achieved the goals of this negotiation.
    c. Incorrect. Often a collaborative approach to a negotiation will take longer due to the time taken in understanding the other party's needs and concerns and then resolving the issue to the benefit of both parties.
    d. Incorrect. This may or may not be the case, depending on the organization's preferred style of negotiating.

94. **Solution: a**
    a. Correct. An analytical person tends to be drawn to details and swayed by factual information.
    b. Incorrect. Pushing an analytical person may result in increased resistance.
    c. Incorrect. Analytical personalities make decisions based on facts rather than on emotions.
    d. Incorrect. The analytical person tends not to enjoy negotiation games as much as other personality types. If the other party believes the negotiator to be deceitful, they may be unwilling to cooperate or even stop negotiations altogether.

95. **Solution: a**
    a. Correct. Without knowing the reason for the resistance, the negotiator is unable to effectively counter it. For example, knowing whether the other party is concerned about the overall issue or a particular piece will impact the negotiator's response.
    b. Incorrect. Generally, a resolution should be attempted at the time. Only if one or both parties to the negotiation need additional time to evaluate new information or calm down should a break be taken.
    c. Incorrect. The negotiator should first work with the other party to determine the cause of disagreement.
    d. Incorrect. Research regarding the other party should occur prior to the initial negotiation meeting.

96. **Solution: c**
    a. Incorrect. These normally arise due to differences in upbringing, cultural and family traditions and socialization process. This source of conflict often becomes highly emotional and takes on moral overtures.
    b. Incorrect. This results from communication breakdown in the organization. This source of conflict is not emotionally charged, and once corrected, there is little resentment.
    c. Correct. This results from intra-individual role conflict and intergroup conflict as a result of functional responsibilities of managers that are interdependent in an interfunctional organization.
    d. Incorrect. These are amplified by a stressful environment where there exists scarce or shrinking resources, downsizing, competitive pressures, or high degrees of uncertainty.

97. **Solution: b**
    a. Incorrect. This is the smoothing style, where goals are conceded in favor of harmony and because it is believed that conflicts damage relationships.
    b. Correct. The withdrawing or avoiding style is viewed as staying away from the issues over which the conflict is taking place and from the people involved in the conflict. It is believed that it is hopeless to try to resolve conflicts and that it is easier to withdraw than face conflict.
    c. Incorrect. This is the forcing style, where opponents are forced to accept the solution. There is no concern with the needs of other people and the negotiation does not care if the solutions are acceptable or not.
    d. Incorrect. This is the confronting style, where solutions are sought to satisfy both parties and maintain relationship. It is also described as a collaborating or win-win style. It involves the conflicting parties meeting face-to-face and collaborating to reach an agreement that satisfies both parties.

98. **Solution: a**
    a. Correct. An avoidance strategy aims to resolve the conflict by ignoring it or imposing a solution. It is appropriate if the conflict is trivial or if quick action is needed to prevent the conflict from arising.
    b. Incorrect. Under a defusion strategy, an attempt is made to deactivate the conflict and to cool the emotions involved. It is appropriate where a temporary measure is needed or when the groups have a mutually important goal.
    c. Incorrect. In a containment strategy, some conflict is allowed to surface but it is carefully contained by spelling out which issues are to be discussed and how are they to be resolved.
    d. Incorrect. In a confrontation strategy, all issues are brought out in the open and conflicting groups directly confront the issues and each other in an attempt to reach a mutually satisfactory solution.

99. **Solution: c**
    a. Incorrect. Traditional negotiation begins when one party approaches another with a proposal that suits their own needs, but when using added-value negotiation, the first party initiating negotiation will provide several proposals.
    b. Incorrect. Added-value negotiations avoid offers and counteroffers by focusing on mutually beneficial solutions.
    c. Correct. When using added-value negotiation techniques, the initiating party always offers several alternatives for negotiation so that the parties may reach a mutually beneficial solution.
    d. Incorrect. When using added-value negotiation techniques, neither party will concede to the demands of the other. Instead, added-value negotiators should make their best offer at the onset of negotiations.

100. **Solution: b (I and III only)**
    I, III. Correct. The principled negotiation method is based on focusing on basic interests, mutually satisfying options, and fair standards. The basic principles include:
      · Separate the people from the problem.
      · Focus on interests, not positions.
      · Invent options for mutual gain.
      · Insist on using objective criteria.
    II, IV. Incorrect. See answers I and III.

END OF PART IV SOLUTIONS